Praise for Jeffrey Yamaguchi and  *Projects*

"*52 Projects* is a creative catalyst that encourages you to find beauty in the mundane things you do every day. And any book that encourages people to experiment until they create the perfect margarita is a winner in my eyes!"

—Karyn Bosnak, author of *Save Karyn*

"Sitting in a cafe reading *52 Projects* I find myself excitedly opening my journal to begin something new, (project #10). This book proves what I have long believed is true, that creative inspiration is contagious. Sometimes all we need is a little reminder that we CAN create no matter what is going on in our current life, no matter what our situation. We need not wait for the ideal situation. *52 Projects* gives us permission to begin NOW, right where you are sitting."

—Keri Smith, author and illustrator
of *Living Out Loud*

"A treasure-trove of inspirational activities, *52 Projects* is everything you'll need to get your creative juices flowing."

—Chris Baty, director of National Novel
Writing Month (NaNoWriMo.org)
and author of *No Plot? No Problem!*

"Thoughtful and inspiring. *52 Projects* will unleash the inner original in all of us."

—Calvin Liu, editor of *Bullfight Review*

"In this little gem of a book is one of the secrets of true happiness. *52 Projects* shows you how to get blissfully lost in time, give priceless gifts that last a lifetime, romp down memory lane, live in the moment but create treasures for the future, and discover your authentic self. All in one book!"

—Susan and Larry Terkel, authors, *Small Change: It's the Little Things in Life That Make a Big Difference!*

"Jeffrey Yamaguchi's *52 Projects* is a heartfelt guide to creating perfect moments and connecting with others. It's a perfect antidote to our zone-out culture—a magical work that will remind you—52 times—how great it is to be alive."

—Dave Isay, public radio producer and founder of StoryCorps

"For those moments when you've hit a creative wall and still aren't sure whether you should go around, over, or under it, completing—or even just reading—some of Yamaguchi's projects can tear you away from the task you've been struggling with and help your creative mind get moving again."

—Andrew Womack, co-publisher, *The Morning News* (themorningnews.org)

"Ours would be a richer world, if every citizen between the ages of 11 and 93 kept a copy of *52 Projects* atop his or her toilet tank, where it could be referred to constantly and spontaneously. Full of high pranking spirits and sentimental recognition of the most deserving stripe, Jeffrey Yamaguchi's suggestions reduced me to tears even as they sent me scuttling for the padded envelope in which I happily mailed my first project to a stranger."

—Ayun Halliday, author of *No Touch Monkey! And Other Travel Lessons Learned Too Late*

"In the hustle bustle of everyday life, being creative in a limited amount of time can be a daunting prospect. *52 Projects* taught me that even seemingly simple ideas can kick start the creative juices."

—Heather Powazek Champ, creator and curator of mirrorproject.com

"Jeffrey Yamaguchi's book is like a magic elixir that can work for anyone. From creative folks in a slump to new artistic hopefuls trying to figure out what the heck to do. *52 Projects* is filled with ideas that are simple and fun, but can result in brilliant and complex art."

—Kevin Sampsell, author, critic, and publisher of Future Tense Books

"*52 Projects* is a grown up activity book for smart, witty, busy people. It's whimsical and practical at the same time. Jeffrey Yamaguchi brings a Fluxus take to the new craft zeitgeist. *52 Projects* helps you channel your creative prowess without subjecting you to any pandering new age crap. A 'self help' book you wouldn't be ashamed to read on the subway. A craft book for people with a college degree. A totally loveable book. I adore it."

—Tsia Carson, editor of SuperNaturale.com

"*52 Projects* is the perfect self-help book for hipsters. It inspires everyone to insert whimsy and creativity into their lives—just the thing we all need to be happy."

—Jean Railla, author of *Get Crafty: Hip Home Ec*

A PERIGEE BOOK

JEFFREY YAMAGUCHI

52

PROJECTS

RANDOM
ACTS
of
EVERYDAY
CREATIVITY

THE BERKLEY PUBLISHING GROUP
Published by the Penguin Group
Penguin Group (USA) Inc.
375 Hudson Street, New York, New York 10014, USA

Penguin Group (Canada), 90 Eglinton Avenue East, Suite 700, Toronto, Ontario M4P 2Y3,
    Canada (a division of Pearson Penguin Canada Inc.)
Penguin Books Ltd., 80 Strand, London WC2R 0RL, England
Penguin Group Ireland, 25 St. Stephen's Green, Dublin 2, Ireland (a division of Penguin Books
    Ltd.)
Penguin Group (Australia), 250 Camberwell Road, Camberwell, Victoria 3124, Australia
(a division of Pearson Australia Group Pty. Ltd.)
Penguin Books India Pvt. Ltd., 11 Community Centre, Panchsheel Park, New Delhi—110 017,
    India
Penguin Group (NZ), cnr. Airborne and Rosedale Roads, Albany, Auckland 1310, New Zealand
    (a division of Pearson New Zealand Ltd.)
Penguin Books (South Africa) (Pty.) Ltd., 24 Sturdee Avenue, Rosebank, Johannesburg 2196,
    South Africa
Penguin Books Ltd., Registered Offices: 80 Strand, London WC2R 0RL, England

PRINTING HISTORY
Perigee trade paperback edition / November 2005

PERIGEE is a registered trademark of Penguin Group (USA) Inc.
The "P" design is a trademark belonging to Penguin Group (USA) Inc.

Library of Congress Cataloging-in-Publication Data

Yamaguchi, Jeffrey
    52 projects / Jeffrey Yamaguchi.
        p. cm.
    "A Perigee Book"
    ISBN 0-399-53206-4
    1. Handicraft. I Title: Fifty-two projects. II. Title.

TT157.Y23 2005
745.5—dc22   2005043255

PRINTED IN THE UNITED STATES OF AMERICA

10 9 8 7 6 5 4 3 2 1

For Juhu
and

my family —Jodie, Scott, Mom, and Dad

ACKNOWLEDGMENTS

I'D LIKE TO THANK all the readers of the *52 Projects* website (which the book was born out of) for the links, the kind words, and the heartfelt letters in which you shared your enthusiasm for project-making and the ways in which your own creative projects have positively impacted your lives. A very special thanks to those who have contributed projects to whatsyourproject.com, which inspire not only me, but all those who come across the site.

Thanks to Sheila Curry Oakes for bringing this book into the house, to John Duff for his support, the designers Ben Gibson, Tiffany Estreicher, and Judith Stagnitto Abbate for making it look so good, and most especially to Michelle Howry, whose enthusiasm, professional flair, and editorial magic have combined to make 52 *Projects* a stronger book. (The very first time I walked into the Penguin offices, it was for a job interview during my first few weeks in New York in 1998. The HR person made me take a typing test on a manual typewriter [well into the age of computers, mind you]. I didn't like that very much, mainly because I didn't just have the guts to walk out. Perhaps I didn't hide that sentiment very well. I did not get the job. Needless to say, I'm so glad I got another chance at Penguin.)

Thanks to Faith Hamlin for the steady hand, the calm force, the knowing insights. I am so grateful for the energy, the guidance, and all that she has done for me and this project. Thanks also to Rebecca Friedman for her keen insights and enthusiastic support of the book.

Thanks to Sangeeta Mehta, Aaron Cheesman, Justin Nisbet, Ada Chu, and Gordon Hurd, true friends who have been there for me, have listened to me ramble on and on (and on), and have always been honest about and supportive of my work, especially with 52 *Projects*.

Thanks to Nana, who wrote me the first long letter I ever received; to my grandparents, whose photos in the basement are all my favorites, and to Aunt Vee, who always ends her cards with a reminder to me and my wife to have fun and love each other.

Thanks to my sister, Jodie, my brother, Scott, and my mom and dad—my family, who have made it so that

I have lived my entire life, every single second, with love and support. That makes creativity, among many others things, thrive and shine through everything that matters and all the rest of it to boot.

And the deepest thanks goes to my wife, Juhu, who, when I would say, "Hey, listen to this new project and tell me what you think," told me, "You should be working on your novel." That's not being mean. That's marriage. On good days and bad, we get that to our core. When my world gets blown to bits or when it all comes together perfectly, I see one person in front of me.

CONTENTS

52 Projects is an eclectic collection of offbeat, exploratory, artistic projects: memory inducing and life-affirming writing exercises; photographic assignments that capture the essence of fleeting moments and times that you wish could last forever; exploration of the arts—from the culinary to the literary; ideas for gifts from the heart; mail art that seals in and delivers the true treasure of friendship; video- and tape-recording schemes that secure for the future an unedited and unfiltered understanding of the past; ideas to document and preserve the little details that make up the life you are living; archeological digs through cluttered drawers and dusty boxes; and adventures that take you to places that you have never been before, even though they're right in front of you.

Beyond a camera and film, pen and paper, and a tape recorder, the only other materials required are intangible: memory, creative energy, and imagination. Skill level and age are irrelevant, and the cost of making the projects ranges from nothing at all to extremely inexpensive. The complexity of the projects is determined by how far you want to take them. The projects can take an hour or a lifetime.

The projects provide a way to take stock of something that has happened in the past; to creatively explore the things that matter to you most in order to figure out where to take your life next; or to turn the run-of-the-mill ordinary into something to celebrate and further enrich your life.

52 Projects is full of "homemade" gift ideas—gifts from the heart. A collection of rainy-day activities. Projects for the creatively blocked. Or the opposite—projects for people who are always on the lookout for a new project to start. A source for scrapbook hobbyists. Ideas to affordably decorate a living space. A cure for the doldrums or an escape from lethargy. A fool-proof system to cut down on television consumption. A compass to get back to places that you've been before, both physically and mentally. A map to the lost scrolls of your long-ago past. Ways to make your special someone feel special. An engine to lift spirits. It is all of these things and more.

In the end, though, *52 Projects* is about what you make it. Remember, the idea of *52 Projects* isn't necessarily for you to re-create these projects exactly. (Following something to the letter is never that much fun.) My hope is that these projects will initiate introspection and the impulse to create and to share. The main idea is for you to be inspired to do projects of your own creation. *52 Projects* serves as a jumping-off point, a spark that ignites the idea, a reminder of the thing that you've been wanting to do.

Photograph yourself at 3 A.M.

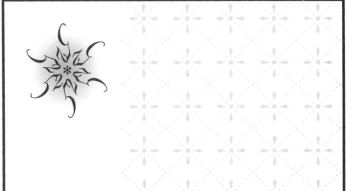

WHY I MAKE PROJECTS

feel the most alive when I am creating something.

I see this, or read that, an old memory suddenly comes to mind from out of nowhere, I have an engaging conversation with a new friend, or have a strange dream—the different influences wrap themselves around each other, get lit up by an underlying stream of energy and a bolt of inspiration, and a project is born. I take the idea and run with it. I start with nothing and keep on working until I have a finished product. I step back and see it there, something of my own creation.

I live for those times when it's well after midnight, and with sore shoulders I'm hunched over the kitchen table working on a project, bleary-eyed but clearly focused on the task at hand, tired but having no desire to hit the sack. Or when I'm on an evening run through the park, huffing and puffing my way through five miles of pavement-pounding exercise, and the only thing I'm thinking about is the concept of my idea for a project—connecting the dots from the list of needed materials to what it looks like at the moment of the unveiling—every other thought and worry pushed aside by the effort to keep on running, keep on breathing, faster and faster, farther and farther, one foot in front of the other as the idea for my project crystallizes and becomes complete in my mind. And of course the feeling I have when I finish a project—despite having to battle back worries that it's no good or that I could've done better—there's a powerful sense that if I put my mind to it, I can do anything, anything at all.

That's why I'm always working on projects. I like the way the process of creating a project makes me feel, the things that I learn, how it energizes and inspires me, the opportunities I find within each step along the way, and, of course, the end result.

When this emphasis on project-making took hold and became a part of my day-to-day life, I'm not exactly sure. There is no defining moment, or rather, project, to pinpoint. It was a gradual process of recognition built over time, one project at a time. What does come to mind, though, is a series of memorable experiences that heavily influenced my concept of projects and laid the foundation for the positive force that project-making has become in my life.

✳ A letter to the editor that my mom wrote years ago, after hearing that one of the local shops had banned the Salvation Army from collecting donations at their entrance during the holiday season because customers had supposedly complained about the ringing of the bell. The letter—one of the most eloquent I have ever read—forcefully argued that it was wrong for the store to hinder such a traditional, charitable effort, and stated that she, along with potentially many other consumers, would be sure to patronize only those stores that made room for the spirit of giving, where the ringing of the bell wasn't an inconvenience, but a beacon of goodwill.

✳ Fifteen minutes of typing, every day, at the typewriters in the library during college. I had just read *On the Road* and was going through the required Jack Kerouac phase. One day, while avoiding my studies at the library, I wandered into a room with a bunch of typewriters. I sat down and began typing for about fifteen minutes straight. I really dug the clanging of the machinery, the punch of each letter and punctuation symbol stamping itself onto the paper, the individual flurry of the tiny metal rods, the way it felt to hit the keys. It was an exercise in simply typing up my thoughts. Occasionally, it

Write down the story of when you rolled lucky 7.

would take the form of a really bad poem, or become the start of a promising story. Those fifteen minutes of writing at the typewriters become a daily habit. It was one of the most liberating writing experiences I have ever had, and the memory of that feeling helps me to this day when I'm sitting in front of a computer, staring at a blank screen.

❈ Pictures or poems or stories, usually all three, on woodwork. Despite lacking any woodworking skills, not to mention the requisite tools and machinery, I began making little boxes and frames. Lots of sandpaper helped even out the edges, but the rough cuts and hard hammering were all too obvious. A master at this I was not, but that didn't stop me from making all manner of these wood-based projects for my wife. I'd glue photographs and write poems or stories all over the pieces. My wife appreciated my efforts, but eventually she was forced to point out that there just wasn't any more room on the shelves. Of course it took me a while to get the hint, and that's why we've got boxes of these things put away in storage.

❈ Rediscovering an old letter from my grandmother, who passed away years ago. What a treasure it is: a ten-page, single-spaced typewritten letter—on old-school translucent typing paper—in which she described in meticulous detail her first and only tour through Europe, day by day.

Write down the story of when you were behind the 8 ball.

 JEFFREY YAMAGUCHI

✳ The family portraits in my grandma and grandfather's basement. Each time I visit, I take a look at all the photos and family portraits, which cover almost every inch of available wall space. It's always striking to see not only pictures of myself as a little boy, but also to see my siblings as infants, as well as my parents when they were so young. My grandfather, who had a long career as a photographer and at the age of eighty-three still works part-time at a photo lab, takes me through the photographs, and he knows the year and story of each one. There's the picture of my grandparents getting married in the internment camp; the picture of my grandmother in downtown Chicago, just weeks after getting out of the camps; the family portrait taken at Christmas time in downtown Chicago, everyone arm in arm; the portrait with the family's first television featured prominently; and the family portrait taken just before my parents and I (a one-year-old at the time) left Illinois and moved to California. I can never pick a favorite because they're *all* my favorites. But my grandfather, he says the individual portraits of his three kids, all taken at different times, are his favorite photographs. "I took these just before they lost their baby fat," he always tells me. "They're growing up, but they haven't quite lost the earliest features of their youth."

✳ The story of my lost adventure as the Wiener Mobile Boy. This was a piece I wrote about my mom's

Document yourself getting dressed to the nines.

nagging effort to get me to apply to be a driver of the famed Oscar Mayer Wiener Mobile, only to have one of the current Wiener Mobile drivers pull into the hotel where my parents were staying on one of their visits to see me. (Oh yes, we met him, got the tour and everything.) And it is this story that in many ways launched my writing career. It was the inspiration for my 'zine, *Working for the Man— Stories from Behind the Cubicle Wall,* which in turn led to the creation of my work humor website— workingfortheman.com. The 'zine and the website gave rise to the *Working for the Man* book, which I self-published. All this effort with the various *Working for the Man* projects caught the attention of a few magazine editors and led to my work getting published in some major magazines. I parlayed those clips into more writing assignments, and even jobs. Perhaps the craziest thing of all is how I used biting work humor—seen by some as antiwork (which would be a rather shallow, misguided take on what *Working for the Man* is all about)—to land some of the best jobs I have ever had and to correct a career trajectory that had really gotten off track.

Describe your perfect 10.

WHAT PROJECTS
DO FOR ME

eeking out, working on, and completing projects impacts me in all kinds of ways. Although I've always held good, professional positions, there have been many points at which I have felt trapped on the wrong career track. Despite hard work and long hours, I found myself feeling completely unfulfilled. That's just the way it is at times regarding work, and I know that I am not alone in feeling this way. But throughout the years of my working life, making projects has helped me get past professional malaise and, on several landmark occasions, into better jobs. I attribute it to the way the creative energy built up around a project ends up seeping into the other parts of my life where energy is lacking.

The truth is, I've really come to depend on the energy that projects give me, and I seek to trigger it when I find myself in a lethargic rut—those times when I'm watching way too much television, endlessly surfing the web in essentially a catatonic state, buying lots of books only to leave them unread on the nightstand, renting too many movies, and picking up lots of takeout. On Friday nights, when I'm too tired to even go out for just a beer at the neighborhood bar. When I'm feeling sorry for myself. When I just don't feel like doing anything at all. What brings this on could be any number of things: bad days at work, tension in my relationships with others, a string of bad luck incidents, getting sick, or hearing some sad news—or it could be nothing in particular: just life wearing me down. What helps me get back up is delving into some kind of project.

Once I buckle down and set to work on a project, the weight of all that sloth is immediately obliterated. It feels as if I'm waking up after a good night's rest and I can just tell, in the way that you sometimes can, that it's going to be a fantastic day.

Along with this surge in energy comes an intensification in my creativity. I'm able to better channel all the thoughts and feelings I have about not only all the sources of inspiration all around me but on my ideas as well. Part of this is simply the result of working on

Write down what eggs are in your basket.

JEFFREY YAMAGUCHI

something in which I have to visualize an entire process from start to finish. But it's also because I am getting to create something on my own terms. I get to truly rely on my own instincts, run with my vision, give it my voice. I establish my own guidelines, and I set the deadlines. I can do whatever I want. I own it, completely. The success is mine, and so is the failure: I possess all the angles and both ends of the spectrum. It's an extremely empowering process, and the more that I engage myself in it, the freer that I feel, in my thoughts, my ideas, and my outlook on the world.

And there is always that next project. For me, projects beget projects. Just being in that project-making mode turns me into a bit of a sponge—everywhere I turn, I see or hear or read about something that inspires me. Working on projects puts my energy into high gear, keeps my creativity flowing, and lets my imagination run wild, and that gives rise to even more complex, challenging, and meaningful projects. It's a cycle of physical and mental momentum, one that I use to keep pushing forward and higher, to places I've never been before.

Write down thirteen of your superstitions.

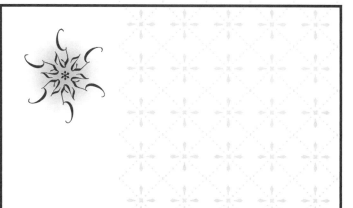

THE STORY
OF *52 PROJECTS*

52 Projects is itself a project: a project about projects. It began as a challenge for myself—to come up with and write down fifty-two projects that I have either done or aspired to complete. I knew that I had lots of ideas for projects—some jotted down in notebooks, others in progress, and many more halfway hatched and stored in the back of my mind. But I had never before attempted to order and organize my project ideas in a formal way. So the game was on.

In early 2002, I began placing the projects on the

web—at www.52projects.com—as often as I came up with a new one. In the beginning, with all kinds of project ideas swirling around in my head, I figured I'd be finished in no time, with plenty of projects to spare. Things changed, however, as I headed toward the halfway point. I started to struggle a bit. It's not that I didn't have any ideas. But questions like, "Is this project good enough?" or "Is this project too similar to something I've already written up?" began to creep into my thoughts. But as I got closer to reaching the magic number fifty-two, I hit a nice, comfortable stride, coming up with project after project—though a new kind of difficulty did emerge: as the number of slots began to diminish, I had to make sure the right projects made the cut. Which to choose? Making the decisions wasn't always so easy.

All along the way, from Project #1 through Project #52, people were visiting the website. You put something up on the web, and people are going to check it out. Somehow, some way, they will stumble upon the site. So from the start, I knew people were going to see the projects. But I was genuinely surprised, and very excited, by the way people were responding to the 52projects.com website.

It all started with a link here and a link there. People with their own websites, blogs, and online journals thought 52projects.com was interesting enough to encourage their own readers to check it out. Links beget more links, and so the number continued to grow.

Hold a parallel parking competition. Document the entire event.

Many of these links would be followed by comments—everything from simply saying things along the lines of "Check out these cool projects" or "If you're bored and looking for something to do, try this site" to much longer entries that explained a project idea of their own that they planned to do. In addition, online media outlets, some small-scale, others quite huge in their reach, began to review the site. The net result of this attention was lots of visits to the site by people from all over the world.

Several of the projects even inspired online communities. Someone out there would take one of the projects, shape and adapt it into something new and different, and then invite and encourage others to participate. I was certainly thrilled to see 52projects.com acknowledged in this way, but was even more excited by the way people were adding in their own energy, enthusiasm, and ideas to essentially make the projects their own.

And then there were the emails that streamed into my Inbox. Now, I've published several websites, and gotten my share of correspondence from people who have come across those sites—the notes range from someone just wanting to let me know they've enjoyed the site to a fellow website publisher asking if I'd like to exchange links. But the notes that came in from people regarding 52projects.com were strikingly different: they were more heartfelt, and much more personal. Some would relay to me how the projects inspired them. Others would tell me what happened once they set to work on a specific project—how it evolved as their own imagination and circumstances entangled themselves in the process. Many people would tell me they were now fired up about getting started on their own project, either one they had always meant to do or one that they had just thought up.

I was extremely moved by these letters, and totally inspired by them. I'd be at my desk, just going through email, deleting all the spam and special offers, when I'd come across one of these notes: and every time, the words—sometimes just one or two lines—would stop me in my tracks. It just felt good to know that 52projects.com was having this kind of positive impact. These letters really brought home the belief that the way the projects had come together had really worked. And not only were people inspired by the projects; just like me, they were seeking out ideas and feeling a need to create from within. What I found most gratifying, and what really energized me, was seeing people who were passionate and enthusiastic and excited, reaching into their own imagination and creativity to make projects on their own terms.

All of the amazing feedback, comments, and letters resulted in the idea for a new component to the 52projects.com website—whatsyourproject.com. It was the perfect, and natural, next step. At this site, people are invited to send in *their* project ideas. Keeping in mind that the goal of 52projects.com is to encourage

Define the way you vote.

individualized project-making, whatsyourproject.com offers up some inspiring proof—by featuring unique, thought-provoking projects contributed by people from all over—that project-making is definitely going on, and splendidly at that. The projects posted are all wonderful, insightful, and generous, and the list continues to grow. (This begs the question: What's your project? More details on how to contribute on page 175.)

What collectively emerged from all this for the 52 *Projects* project is the book that you are reading right now. I've taken the original projects from the 52projects.com website, added quite a few more, and further explored how projects can impact not only your creative endeavors, but your life in general. But the main point of the original idea remains: You aren't supposed to make these projects exactly as written. Though this book is just one of the endless ways to trigger your imagination, juice up your creativity, and discover or rediscover your muses, the hope is that the personal exploration of project-making that it encourages will inspire you to dream up, set to work on, and complete projects that are all your own.

Write down the first memory that comes to mind from when you were nineteen years old.

PROJECTS ARE FOR YOU

There's no way around it: We're always involved in some kind of project. Whether it's making a gift for a friend, the need to decorate a new pad, killing some time and stamping out the boredom, or simply getting an idea and working to put the pieces together, we've always got something on the drawing boards of our minds, not to mention our kitchen tables. Following is a list of reasons why project-making slips into our lives, whether we like it or not.

※ You have to get a gift for a friend, but you are tired of going the typical routes—candle holders, cool frames, nice-smelling soaps, or the oft-given, totally impersonal music store gift certificate. You want to create something very personal.

※ Everyone else is bringing a bottle of wine to the housewarming party, but you want to bring something that really warms the house.

※ You've gotten into the routine of waking up, going to work, coming home, fixing a quick dinner, watching television until it's time to go to bed, only to wake up and do the exact same thing all over again. You want out of that routine.

※ You're constantly on the road, spending lots of time in planes, at airports, and in hotel rooms (watching CNN Headline News and bad movies, the occasional porn flick when you feel like you can slip the charge by Accounting). You don't want to pop open the laptop and work on spreadsheets. You want to use the time wisely and you want to be productive— not for the company, but for yourself.

※ You are a scrapbook hobbyist, and you are always on the hunt for new, creative ideas.

✳ You mail cards for every occasion to friends, family, coworkers, and others. You don't want a card company to say it for you.

✳ It's Sunday afternoon, raining outside, and there's nothing on TV except infomercials.

✳ You get home from work and you're too tired to do much of anything, but you refuse to sit in front of the television all night and watch *Law & Order* reruns.

✳ You go to a museum, and all you want to do when you get home is paint.

✳ You get inspired, by a movie or something you've read or some song or a latenight conversation, and instead of sleeping on it, you work on whatever it is that you're working on until the crack of dawn, your bleary eyes stinging and red, your back aching, but your mind just whirling along with an energy that only comes when true inspiration hits.

✳ You may not say it out loud, you may not even admit it to your closest friends, but you consider yourself an artist.

✳ You watch cooking shows on television, but instead of saying, "Man, that sure looked good" (perhaps while reaching for a jar of spaghetti sauce), you ac-

Put stamps on random pieces of paper (cut to postcard size) and mail them off.

tually go into the kitchen and attempt to cook the meals you saw prepared by the professional chefs.

※ You've got a law degree and a great job, but what you really want to be is a furniture designer.

※ Your accounting job pays the bills, but what you truly love to do is make jewelry.

※ You don't just zone out while on public transportation: you write in your journal, knit, or work on your novel/play/screenplay.

※ You regularly write poems to your significant other (well beyond the first swooning six weeks at the beginning of the relationship).

※ You want to do something more with your photos than simply put them in frames and photo albums.

※ You like throwing parties with interesting twists.

※ You're always writing ideas in your journal.

※ You want to leave something for family and friends to remember you by.

※ You can't afford art from a gallery.

✳ You can afford art from a gallery, but it just doesn't speak to you.

✳ You are simply always on the lookout for new projects.

✳ You're always on the hunt for projects to keep your kids busy, or for projects to do with your kids.

✳ One of your favorite things to do is go to a craft or art store, walk the aisles, and think about all the cool stuff you can make.

✳ You can come up with an idea and build a website over a weekend.

✳ You're constantly posting your thoughts and insights and stories on your online journal.

✳ You buy arts-and-crafts and home design magazines, flag the pages with stuff you like, but that's as far as you get. Or you flag the pages and for the next few weeks, you're busy working on new projects.

✳ You keep taking the mix-tape concept further and further.

✳ You are proficient at making company time your time, meaning you never get caught doing personal, nonwork-related work while you are on the clock.

Write down your most vivid Christmas memory.

WHAT PROJECTS CAN DO FOR YOU

It's not just about the final product. Making projects takes you through an entire creative process, one that taps into who you are; the people, places, and things that influence you; where you've been, and where you are going to next; how you see the world and what you're feeling on the inside. Delving into this process again and again stretches your imagination, generates new sources of energy, enhances your creative outlook and mindset, and continually pushes the limits of your skills and talents. The impact of all this project-making

is far-reaching: Not only will it improve the next project you decide to make but also how you go about
making your way through the day-to-day business of life.

✳ Projects are a major source of energy.

It's all about momentum. The more you engage
your mind and follow through on your ideas, the easier
it is to come up with and build creative projects. All that
energy just feeds off itself and continues to grow. Even
if you screw up, the energy is there to keep you going
forward. If your project is going according to plan, it
helps you see ways to improve it and make it even more
amazing. But most important, the energy establishes
the mental and emotional space to allow your ideas to
lead to other ideas, and projects lead to other projects.
That energy finds all kinds of ways to manifest itself in
every part of your life. An underlying sense that you can
do anything you put your mind to also pervades your
outlook on life in general.

✳ Projects help you deal with your job.

Man, the grind. Regardless of whether you've got a
great job that fulfills you or a job that you can barely
drag yourself out of bed to get to, work has a way of

wearing you down and fraying your nerves. It might be cyclical, an up-and-down thing, or it can be something that happens gradually, a long, downward slide toward being totally disgruntled and miserable. It's all the usual culprits: the stress of deadlines, dealing with coworkers and the boss, the long hours, and all of the other work-related BS. Underneath it all is that while you own your work, there are a lot of other voices and orders and demands that guide what you do and how you do it. And let's face it, no matter what job you currently have, whether it's a job you like or not, there's always that dream job off in the distance.

Projects provide an outlet that you own completely—you get to make all the decisions. You're not doing the work because it's been assigned, and it's not just about getting the approval of your boss or the board. That can be quite liberating. Your creativity and imagination can run wild, and the more you step into your own unique visions, the bigger the pictures get.

If you let your work get to you, so much so that you come home every night pissed off and wanting to do nothing more than veg out in front of the television, the momentum moves in the opposite direction—the visions pitter out and the shrinking, solitary picture in your frazzled mind fades to static. And the longer you sit there and do nothing, the more tired and empty you will feel. But if you're building something of your own design, the ideas will be flowing and your mind will be whirling and you won't quit when it's all over: You'll be raring to go on the next project, something bigger and better and more complex than the one before. That momentum is bound to spill over into everything else that you do, including how you approach your duties and responsibilities in the workplace.

And though you can't expect to be able to quit your job immediately and start making a living as a photographer, or writer, or painter, or whatever art form your projects involve, your project-making efforts will definitely inspire you to seek out opportunities that are more in line with what it is that you truly love to do, whether those are within your present company, at a new job, or in an entirely new career.

✳ Projects make you feel better about yourself.

Turn off the television, stop bitching and moaning to whomever it is on the other end of the phone line, and make sure you get your ass out of bed before noon. Instead of being slothful and hanging yourself with a "poor me" attitude, get busy on some projects. Why? Because making projects is an excellent way to prop yourself up when you aren't feeling so good about where you're at in your life. You simply cannot underestimate the power of a sense of accomplishment. You may not be close to finishing that three hundred—page novel, but you can get some kind of cool project done—and once you put the final touches on even a lower-scale project, damn, if you won't feel like you will get that three hundred–page novel done in no time.

Take this effort one step further and make projects with other people in mind, to give to them as gifts. Not only do you get the satisfaction of completing projects, but you put big smiles on other people's faces. Such acts of kindness go a long way. Knowing that you've brought some happiness to others is going to give you one of those wonderful highs that makes you feel like 1) The world ain't such a bad place after all; 2) It's time to just move on from whatever it is that's dragging you down; and 3) You're ready to take on whatever life throws in front of you. It's a good place to be.

✻ Projects make your close friends, family, and significant other feel truly special.

How often do you hear someone say, "Wow, an actual letter, and not an email!" when they get a handwritten note in the mail? It really is that simple to make someone's day. Going beyond birthdays and the usual holiday exchanges, presenting a gift of your own creation just out of the blue is the way to have the biggest impact. And of course, gift-giving does not have to be confined to the people in your circle. There's something magical about leaving an artistic footprint in the form of a project for people whom you don't know and

Track down pictures of all your Halloween costumes.

will never meet. While you know you are making a positive contribution, the mystery of the unknown makes the possibilities of the impact seem endless.

✻ Just like the projects of others inspire you, your projects inspire others.

You know from your own experience how the engaging work of others—that you see firsthand or even just read about in the newspaper—gets your creative juices flowing and pushes you to get going on your own projects. So it makes total sense that the work you create can have the same effect on others. Putting projects out there can't help but set in motion an expanding cycle of energy, goodwill, and inspiration.

✻ Projects can save you money.

It's no secret that going the way of the homemade is much less expensive than going to the store and buying something ready-made. A store-bought card alone can set you back some serious dollars these days. And though you might be spending less money or no money at all, projects that you plan to give as gifts will have a worth that surpasses even the greatest of monetary values.

Document the first day it drops below thirty-two degrees.

✳ Projects help you deal with mistakes.

Whatever you envision in terms of how your finished project is going to look, it most likely won't turn
out that way. Best-laid plans . . . you know how those
go. Variables come into play. Something that seemed
like it would be very easy turns out to be anything but.
Screw-ups occur and are bound to happen, and that's
just part of the deal. If you mess up, of course you're
going to get angry, possibly storm out of the room and
announce that you've quit whatever it is that you've
been working on. I think that's just part of the creative
process—you'll hit that point time and time again with
each project that you make. Keep up the good fight:
The more projects that you make, the easier it will become to find solutions in spite of miscalculations, work
around the mistakes, and manage the inevitable crises.

**✳ Projects help you overcome the fear
of failure.**

Sometimes just the idea of making a mistake—the
fear of failure—can keep you from even embarking on a
project. But the more projects you create, the easier it

will become to simply see past the fear. Each time you go through the process of coming up with an idea and working through the steps of making it a reality, the more secure you will become in your own creativity and unique project-making abilities. You know that if you simply buckle down and follow through from start to finish, you will get your project done. Failure won't be an option—it won't even cross your mind.

✱ Projects help you deal with insecurity.

Of course we are usually the harshest critics of our own work, but there is another variation on fear that can act as a deterrent to getting started on a project, and that is the fear that other people might not like what we've created. It's natural to wonder if something we have made is any good. In the worst-case scenario, I suppose we picture someone pointing at our project, barely able to ask, "What is *that*?" through cackling laughter. That's just letting your insecurities get the best of you. And even if that did happen, because let's face it, there's always a chance that you're going to create a real mess of a project, you will survive and live to make more projects. More than likely, though, people will not only be impressed with what you have made, but will also be impressed by you as a person—someone who had the guts to make something and put it out there for others

Mail a self-addressed, stamped envelope to a friend and tell him or her to send you something.

to see. It does take guts. And the more projects you make and reveal to the world, the tougher you are going to get.

✳ Projects get you involved in community.

Whether it's online, in arts groups, book clubs, knitting circles, photography clubs, writers' groups, or with the community at large, making projects inspires you to seek out people with similar interests—to share your work, exchange information and ideas, and to celebrate whatever craft you happen to be focusing on. The more people that you meet, the more fired up you will be to work on and share your own projects. You'll also be more inspired to get involved in and help grow the communities that you become a part of.

✳ Projects may bring in a little money.

You might just create a project that people are willing to pay money for, whether that's your intention or not. It's probably not a good idea to quit your day job until such interest goes well beyond close friends and family, but if you believe in it and you're willing to do the research and legwork, why the heck not try to take your project to market? It may turn into a full-fledged business, or something you just sell here and there, perhaps at local craft shows during the holiday season. Of course, there's always a chance all your work will end up stowed away in the garage . . . but you never know. You may end up lining your pockets, or you may earn a little extra pocket change; or you could even lose your shirt. As long as you have no delusions about striking it rich and you're enjoying yourself (and you know the difference between revenue and profit), I say go for it.

✳ Projects lead to self-discovery.

A lot of yourself goes into the projects you make. Most fascinating are the surprises that come about during the process—forgotten memories that pop to the forefront of your mind, the sudden, urgent impulse to get in touch with an old friend, remembering how much you used to enjoy taking pictures or reworking your poems over and over again. You might peel back some of the layers you've built up around certain thoughts and feelings and be reminded how important something is to you, even though you haven't given it much thought in a very long time. Working through a project always presents new challenges, and you might realize that you've got gifts and talents, or at least the hint of potential, in something you have never done before. The truth is, each day we learn new things about ourselves.

Shoot a roll of 36-exposure film with a specific project in mind.

But the introspective nature of coming up with and then making a project—with its collusion of unique, personal reference points, creativity, and inspiration—helps to shed some light on these types of revelations.

✳ Projects unleash your creativity.

We're all creative, in our own unique ways, in pretty much everything that we do. We usually just don't take the time to notice. The point is, it's there, in us, from day one. Strangely, there are people out there who think either 1) They're not creative at all, or 2) They don't have any good ideas. That's just hogwash, plain and simple. What is true is that your ideas can get shut out, blocked by the neverending stream of distractions—bad television, a jerkball boss, looming credit card bills, crying kids, dinner menus, work deadlines, oil changes, food shopping, etc., etc., etc. Working on a project can help break through the obstacles and, due to the nature of the project-making process, taps directly into the creativity that is right there, where it has always been and will always be. The more projects you make, the more constant and forceful your creative impulses will be, not only with projects, but the rest of everything else as well.

✳ Projects enhance your skills and talents.

This includes skills and talents you don't even know you have. You may not ever be a master painter, but that shouldn't stop you from picking up a paintbrush. Inherent in the project-making process is the fact that the more you practice a skill, the better you will get at it. The freedom to create on your own terms also opens up some wonderful possibilities. No one is there to tell you that you can't do something, that you aren't qualified, that you aren't right for the job. It's all up to you to figure it out, dig deep, and take some chances. And of course sometimes, when it's all on you, you have no choice but to give it a whirl, despite your lack of experience or knowledge. The results, which may very well include total failure, only mean that you have taken a step in the right direction. Keep on at it, and you are sure to enhance what you can do and how well you do it.

✳ Projects give you a sense of accomplishment.

There is a tremendous amount of power in the sense of accomplishment one feels after making a project. The process of coming up with an idea and seeing it through to completion instills a fiery burst of energy that not only inspires the next great idea, but improves the way you make your way through the day-to-day business of life. So much of what we're required to do is on someone else's terms. It can suck the life out of not only your creativity, but your will to take on things at home, at work, in your relationships, and everything else in between with strength and the full-force of your energy. Setting to work on projects of your own choosing and accomplishing what you set out to create—all on your own terms—helps you to seize, in a positive way, ownership of everything else in your life—even those things that you don't ask for, don't want, have no interest in, and have no choice about.

✳ Projects preserve your memories.

If you're making projects, you can't help but use the pieces of your life. Whether it's something tangible, like old photographs, or something intangible, like the way you feel upon viewing your front yard after the winter's first snow, the things that you experience, the people you meet, the places you go—all find their way into your projects, either directly or indirectly. By default, then, when you make a project you are documenting particular moments from specific periods in your life. The projects you make preserve your memories of

Write down if this is where you thought your life would be.

those times and provide a direct link, by way of your heart and mind, to what you were thinking and feeling from the days of your past.

✳ Projects help you with long-term projects.

Let's say you're already working on a project, something you've been focusing on for years and isn't anywhere close to being finished. When working on a project of this magnitude, sometimes it feels like you're never going to get it done, and it really weighs you down. Finishing the project feels completely out of reach, so much so that instead of barreling into the work at hand, you avoid it. That, in turn, makes you feel guilty. The negativity spirals out of control and ties you up into a state of total paralysis. One way to break out of a rut like this is to get busy on project of a smaller scale, one where you can clearly see the beginning and the end. Going through the process of creation—one where you see the fruits of your labor—helps get the creative juices flowing and gives you a sense of accomplishment. Such an effort will inspire you to get back to work and back on track with your larger-scale, longer-term project, all with renewed vigor.

Record how old you feel.

✳ Projects help you figure out what your long-term project should be.

It's difficult to conceptualize and commit to a single project that you know is going to take an extended period of time. That kind of investment requires confidence in both the idea and the belief that you are going to see it through—two things that go hand in hand. If the idea is shaky, then eventually your commitment to it will falter. Working on projects over time helps you to pick up on both the value and viability of your ideas: You'll know deep down when you've come up with a truly amazing project idea worth a long-haul effort, and you will have the experience to know what it will take to get the job done.

✳ Projects help you come up with even more project ideas.

While working on a project, it's inevitable that ideas for other projects will come to mind. The ideas may be related to the project at hand—an offshoot, perhaps a Part Two—or they may be entirely different in concept and scope. The momentum of your project-making activity simply puts you in a more creative frame of mind. Just make sure that you don't have too many projects going at once so that none of them actually get completed, and don't get in the habit of abandoning a project-in-progress just to start on a new one. One other thing: Don't trust your memory. If you think up a great idea for a new project, write it down. With so many ideas flowing through your head, it's not easy to simply recall from memory every single project that you dream up.

I'm sure hoping that some of the things I've outlined
and discussed make sense and apply to you. But no doubt
you've got your own ideas about what projects can do for
you, even if you've never thought about it in exactly those
terms. Fittingly, figuring out what projects do for you
provides an opportunity for any number of projects:

✳ Write about a project that you've done in the past,
and how it impacted your life.

✳ Write about a project you made and gave as a gift that really made someone's day.

✳ Take or find photographs of all the projects you have created. Assemble the photos into a booklet.

✳ Write the story of the last project you completed: how you came up with the idea, the process you used to create it, any hitches that came up along the way, what it felt like to finish, and what the project means to you.

This list of what projects can do for you never really ends. Each project that you make will present new revelations, and the more projects that you create, the more that project-making will do for you.

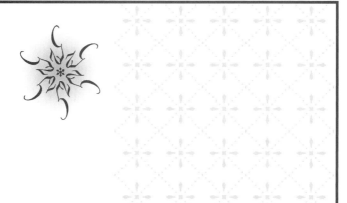

HOW TO USE
52 PROJECTS THE BOOK

You can run with it any way you want to. That's what's so special about this book—the magic comes from *you* and your own unique creative ideas and project-making abilities.

The fifty-two projects in this book are not confined to a specific form of art or subject—they are not just focused on painting or writing or weekend gardening endeavors. The projects are wide open—things that you can do regardless of your age, the resources you have at your disposal, or your skill level.

Each project provides enough information for you to complete it as written. But there is also enough space within each project's basic guidelines to allow you to create something that is truly your own. There is no step 1, step 2, step 3—no picture of a finished project that must be emulated and achieved. You get to visualize your own complete project, letting your imagination and memories and muses guide the creation of whatever it is that you decide to make for yourself or for others.

You can start at Project #1 and keep going until you reach Project #52. You could do one a week for an entire year, using the book as a guide to a very productive year. You can use the book as a constant reminder to get to work on that project you've been meaning to create. You can flip through the pages and skip around until you find a project that jumps out at you and immediately brings to mind a cool, inventive idea of your own. Once you're finished with that project you can open up and thumb through the book again, fired up and ready to create your next project. You can read #1 through #52 straight through, then close your eyes and see all the pieces of your next great idea come together in your mind.

The main thing is to get started right now on your project-making ventures in the way that's right for you. So without further ado, here are the fifty-two projects.

FIND YOUR OLD LETTERS. Gather up all of the letters that one of your oldest friends has sent to you over the years. Photocopy the letters. Put the photocopies in an envelope, and then mail off the envelope to your friend.

PROJECT

1

In high school, one of my best friends and I had Latin class together. Why we were taking Latin when everyone else was smart enough to be taking Spanish or French, I have no idea. I think I was taking Latin because it was going to help me do better on the SAT. Somebody obviously gave me horrible advice. Probably a career counselor. Anyway, Latin was just about the most boring class there ever was. The hour-long period seemed to go on for about two hundred years. The only way my friend and I could stay awake was by writing each other letters. Of course, my friend would still often fall asleep, and a memory of him being jarred awake by the teacher can still get me rolling on the floor:

"T., could you please answer number 15," the teacher

asked my friend. Since T. was sound asleep, he didn't respond. For a very long time. But the mounting stares must have finally gotten to him, because he eventually snapped out of his nap as if being jolted by a live wire. Then he frantically began to flip the pages of his notebook, chanting a steady "Ummmm, uhhhh. Okay, uhhhh . . . Ummmm . . ." to stall and give the pretense that he was on the verge of answering the question. But T. finally had to admit what we all already knew. He had no idea what the teacher had been going over, no idea whatsoever, and finally had to ask, "Ummmm . . . What page are we on?"

Anyway, about eight years after we graduated from high school, I found these letters. So I gathered them up, made copies, and sent them off to my friend. T. wrote me back right away. It was like being thrown back in time and being put face-to-face with his ol' high school self, he wrote in the letter he sent back to me. And he also apologized for something. I remembered exactly what he was referring to. One day I had shown up at school wearing this gold chain with a gold cougar medallion attached to it. Obviously, I was just trying too hard to be different and get some attention, but I did kind of dig this chain. In one of the letters, T.'s reaction to the chain is recorded. He wrote, "And Jeff, what is up with that chain. Why are you wearing it? What message does it convey? I'll tell you what it conveys: 'Jeff is an idiot.'" He read that and felt so horrible about what he had written all those years ago that he wrote me a very serious, heartfelt apology, and he told me he would never, ever do something like that again.

FIND A RECIPE FOR KEY LIME PIE. If you've already got a favorite recipe for key lime pie, even better. Make the pie. Take pictures of the pie. Invite some friends over, and take pictures of them eating the pie. Have a friend take a picture of you eating the pie.

Next, get a box and some limes. Put the limes in the box, along with a handwritten copy of the key lime pie recipe and the pictures that were taken of your key lime pie party. Mail off the box to a friend.

I got this idea from Robert Rauschenberg. I saw a documentary on him, and one of the people interviewed said he had once gotten a box of limes and a recipe for key lime pie from the artist. I watched this whole documentary on Rauschenberg, all about his art and life as an artist. I mean Rauschenberg has been making all this great, groundbreaking work for decades, *and the box of limes is what sticks out in my mind.*

GET YOUR CAMERA. Get on the train. Take the train to the end of the line. Take photos.

3

Interview a couple that has been married for fifty years.

THINK OF YOUR FAVORITE BOOK. Then, go to the library and seek out other books written by the same author.

If F. Scott Fitzgerald's *The Great Gatsby* is your favorite book, check out *Tender Is the Night*. Maybe you

4 PROJECT

loved John Irving's *The World According to Garp*, but have you read *The Water-Method Man*? Steinbeck's *The Grapes of Wrath*, of course, but what about *Travels with Charley* or *The Moon Is Down*? Read Zora Neale Hurston's *Their Eyes Were Watching God*? Well how about *Dust Tracks on a Road*, *Jonah's Gourd Vine*, or *Tell My Horse*. Intrigued by Po Bronson's *The Nudist on the Late Shift*? Check out his first book, *Bombardiers*. Maybe you've only read Janette Turner Hospital's *Oyster*, but she's got a shelf of books—*Borderline*, *The Tiger in the Tiger Pit*, *Charades*, *Isobars*, *Dislocations* . . .

You get the picture.

Write down your UFO sighting story.

MAKE SOME ART, maybe a photograph or a painting or a drawing. Put the art in a nice frame, one that
isn't brand-new. Then, hang your framed art in a place
you aren't supposed to, but where people will assume it
is supposed to be, like the lobby of your apartment build-

5

ing, in the hallway at your office, on the smallest wall in
a motel room, in the quiet corner of a library, outside
the downstair's restroom at a restaurant or bar, the back
room of a club, or in the bathroom of a museum.

Go to 52projects.com, but also, spell it out.

YOU NEVER KNOW when it might all end. That thing about just walking across the street and getting hit by a bus—it really could happen.

6

When I was in college, my girlfriend at the time, H., told me that she was once digging around in her parents' desk drawers, and she came across a letter that was addressed to her, so she opened it. It was a letter from her mother, and it was indeed for H., but it wasn't supposed to be given to H. unless her mother had died. H. realized that after reading just the first sentence, but she kept reading. Of course.

I, of course, asked H. what the letter said. She told me. I wouldn't even think of divulging the contents. That letter was for H., and H. only. I admit I felt a little strange asking and then having her tell me what was in the letter, but it's the kind of thing you open up about with a lover in the middle of the night. I can say that when I asked H. how she responded to reading the letter, she said, simply: "I just started bawling."

A letter like that, it's one of those things that's hard just to think about, let alone actually write up and then seal in an envelope. Making a will is easy. But a letter, to be delivered in the event of your death, to the most important person in your life?

Still, if you sit down, with a pen in hand and paper in front of you, you can do it. So get your affairs in order.

CALL A FRIEND, just to shoot the breeze and catch up. Record the conversation. Make sure to tell your friend what you are doing, but be kind of vague about why you are doing it. Say it's a personal audio journal that you're working on, then quickly change the subject. (If your friend is likely to end up in court or face an in-

PROJECT

7

dependent prosecutor, pick a different friend to record. If something incriminating is said, destroy the tape.)

After the conversation is over, label the tape, with your friend's first name and the date. Then, put the tape in a secure place where it won't be lost forever, but won't be found for years.

When you come across the tape in a few years, during a move or something like that, give the tape to your friend. Once he hears it, he'll say something like, "I can't believe I sound like that on tape," or "I hate the way I sound on tape." But he'll really be shocked at the things he was saying, all those years ago.

Write down the story of your first speeding ticket.

MAKE A POSTER. It can be sized however you want, but 8½" x 11" is easiest to copy and post. In terms of what should be on your poster, that's wide open. The poster can be political, it can promote something you need to get the word out about, it can feature your art,

PROJECT

8

or it can just be something that looks cool and is totally nonsensical. Anything. Once your poster is done, post it all over. You can post it all over a room, an office, a building, a school, a campus, a town, a city, a state, a nation, the world.

During student council elections in my senior year at high school, someone postered the school with scandalous posters. These suckers weren't just put up with tape and tacks. These posters were sealed on with glue. And they were everywhere.

The posters—all featuring various students running for

office—contained crudely drawn characters doing crude things, and the comments were even harsher. Of course everyone thought they were the funniest thing ever.

"DON'T VOTE FOR MIKE, HE SUCKS DICK."

Or

"DON'T VOTE FOR SUSAN, SHE'S A BROWNNOSER."

And all the pictures—a notch above stick-figure drawings—were literal depictions of the comments.

The striking thing was how these posters took aim at all the popular kids, the ones who always seemed to get all the glory and got good grades as well—you know, the kids who end up on student council. Everything always seems to go right for these popular kids—they've got the best clothes, they're good at sports, they have shiny new cars, they run with the best-looking crowd, and they always have the best-looking girlfriends or boyfriends.

The people running for office who actually deserved to win but probably wouldn't were not featured in any of the posters.

So these posters were an attack on the high school hierarchy. And there was indeed some subtle ground-leveling that took place on that day.

"Did you see the one with the . . . ?"

"These things are everywhere!"

"Oh man, this is great!"

And of course, the main focus: "Who do you think did it?"

Usually in situations like this, the person who does the job ends up telling people, or maybe just one person. Then that person tells someone, and that person tells someone, and before you know it, the kid who did the job is sitting in the principal's office waiting for his parents to come pick him up. Busted.

But the person who postered the school must never have told anyone. No one was ever caught, and we never did find out who put up those posters.

THE NEXT TIME you or somebody else breaks a glass in your home, instead of throwing out the smashed pieces, collect the remnants, carefully clean them, and then place them in a jar. Then, label the jar with the time and date that the glass broke, what you (or whoever) had

9 PROJECT

been drinking, who was in your home, the occasion (possibly a birthday party, maybe just "hanging out," most likely "drinking a glass of water—I was thirsty"), exactly how the glass broke, and, of course, the name of the person who broke it. Then, put the sealed and labeled jar on a shelf.

A glass that breaks during a party is the best kind to save. After all, it isn't really a party until something gets broken.

WRITE THE STORY of why you moved to the city in which you currently live.

10

About a year after moving to New York, I read a story entitled "Goodbye to All That" by Joan Didion. It struck a chord with me. I asked my wife to read it, and kept bothering her about it until she finally did. I made copies of the story and gave them out to friends. Didion's story is all about moving to, living in, and then leaving New York, about her experiences in the city, and how those growing experiences eventually lead her to depart. Trying to unravel the mystery of exactly when she decides it's time to move on is the point of the story. The way she writes, it's like she's telling the story in a depressed whisper, but she knows how to rhythmically throw in that deceptively simple, yet perfect sentence that seems to summarize exactly, and I mean exactly, what is going on—not just with her, but with your feelings as well.

More than anything, though, I just like the idea of this story, of putting down on paper why you moved to the city in which you currently live. Why you left where you used to live, what you like about your new home, what that first night was like, the feeling you had the moment you stepped off the plane or drove across the bridge . . . It will all end up finding its way into the story. You build your life, and a lot of what you build it with has to do with where you're living. The reasons why you move to a new city can reveal the undercurrents of how you are trying to shape and direct the course of your life.

SHOTGUN A BEER with your old drinking buddies. Get a twelve-pack of the cheap shit you used to drink back in the day. Then, mail a can to each of your old drinking buddies, as they no doubt live all over the country. In each of the packages, include a note explaining

11

that everyone needs to shotgun their beer at the same time on a specific date. Nothing like the old days, of course, but it will definitely stir up the ol' memories, no matter how hazy those memories might be.

And, man, those were the days. You'd make the call to your connection, maybe someone's older sister's ex-boyfriend, or possibly some guy named Hank who lived in the run-down apartment complex on the other side of town who'd buy your booze for the price of six-pack ("We want 15 twelve-packs of Schaefer and 12 two-liters of Tropical California Cooler"). The exchange would be made, maybe in the back of a supermarket, and the al-

cohol would make it back to the party house and immediately be passed around. To commemorate the start of the party, your best buddies would gather around, use a key or a pocket knife to poke a hole in the side of their beer cans, hoist up the beers, pop the lids, and effectively shotgun the brewskis. The long gulp, then an even longer belch, all in unison. Someone would turn up the song on the stereo, maybe David Bowie's "Changes," "Strangers When We Meet" by the Smithereens, or "Add It Up" by the Violent Femmes, the next round of Schaefer's ("The one beer to have when you're having more than one") would already be in hand, and the party would commence.

TAKE SOME PICTURES of your lover while she's sleeping. Then, write down some dreams.

You can either ask her what she's been dreaming about lately and write those dreams down, or you can write down the dreams that you want her to have. Sweet

dreams. Pleasant dreams. Wet dreams. The kind of dreams that you don't want to wake up from, but when you do, you've got a smile on your face, even if you can't really remember what you were dreaming about.

Once you've got the photos and some dreams written down, frame the photos and the dreams, or make a little book out of them. Then, put your creation under her pillow so that she finds it right as she's going to bed.

Write a letter to your sixty-four-year-old self.

HELP YOUR FRIENDS GET LUCKY.

Have a dinner party on the next Friday the 13th. Invite all of your good friends. At the end of the meal, no matter what kind of cuisine you've served, bring out a tray of fortune cookies.

Make sure to organize the tray so that you know who gets which fortune cookie. The reason for this is because earlier in the day, you carefully pulled out whatever fortunes were in the cookies and replaced them with fortunes specific for each of your friends. You know them well enough to craft just the perfect individualized fortunes: "Monica, you will lose your writer's block and will write the perfect ending to your novel-in-progress," or "John, you will pass the bar exam, no problem," or "Alex, your trip to Europe is going to be full of adventure and will include not just sex, but sexual options,"

Envision your retirement.

or "Sam, those boots you just bought are going to quadruple your already potent knockout status."

7 VARIATIONS ON PROJECT #13

1. Write a very short story about a person having good luck after finding a penny on the street. Make copies of the story and stuff the copies into small envelopes. Tape a penny to the envelopes. Then, walk around and drop the envelopes onto the ground in random places with heavy foot traffic.

2. Have a party on the next Friday the 13th. Sneak into your bedroom, where all the guests' coats are piled high on your bed, and put a $2 bill in each person's pocket.

3. Think about which of your friends is the most down on his luck. On Friday the 13th, pick up something that person needs—and not something that's just functional. It should be something that's fun as well, a gift that will bring out some joy. Wrap it up elaborately, with celebratory effect. Then, go to this person's house under cover of darkness. Go to the front door with the step of a wild beast approaching prey. Leave the gift on the doorstep. Position yourself for a speedy exit. Then, ring the doorbell and run like the wind. Don't look back. Don't ask any questions the next time you see your

Map out your ideal road trip.

friend. Don't tell people what you did. Just let it be. It's guaranteed to bring a smile to your face whenever you think about it.

4. Write down the stories of all your lucky charms. Bind up the stories and distribute on Friday the 13th.

5. Take pictures of your finger pushing the thirteenth-floor button in every elevator you get into over a set period of time. On Friday the 13th, tape these photos onto the walls of as many elevators as you can ride.

6. Make a list of thirteen friends. Call or email them individually. Ask each one about a memory from when they were thirteen years old. If you call them, record the conversation (with their permission, of course). If you email them, make sure they write out the memory so that it reveals as much detail as possible—it may take a few follow-up emails to draw it all out. Then, on Friday the 13th, throw a party and invite your thirteen friends. Give each friend their tape or the words that they wrote.

7. Find pictures of friends that capture an image of when they were lucky: a picture of a friend at the party where he met his current significant other; the day he got his cast off; or what the car looked like after an accident in which no one was injured. It could be an image of your friend catching a fish, scoring a goal, surviving a particularly dangerous ski jump. It could be any number of situations. We tend to get lucky more than we think we do.

It's really about going through all those stacks of photos to find the images that capture these times when good luck is striking hot. Once you find them, and they will be there—we tend to take pictures during moments in which smiles are the natural reaction, and surely good luck has to occasionally factor into these times of happiness—mail them off to your friends so that they receive them on Friday the 13th. They will feel doubly lucky, especially if Friday the 13th happens to fall on a night with a full moon.

WRITE DOWN the lyrics to your favorite songs. Sometimes, you know all the words by heart. Other

14

times you don't know more than a few lines, especially if any of your favorite songs are by Tom Waits. Then there are songs where you know most of the lines, pretty much all of them, except for a few mystery phrases that you just can't quite decipher, even after thousands of late-night performances in your underwear in front of the mirror. A little research may be required, but it's worth it: You'll definitely get a kick out of actually writing out the complete lyrics of a favorite song and seeing the words laid bare on paper. It's surprising to see how they can either read like beautiful, layered, masterful poetry (such as Tom Waits's "Who Are You") or, on the

Turn a project on its head.

other side of the spectrum, the poetry of a ninth grader (like Queen and David Bowie's "Under Pressure").

It really is the music that makes lyrics work. "Jump" by Van Halen sounds like a cool rock song. Aztec Camera's version of "Jump" sounds like an anthem, mood and memory and all the rest of it flowing through your mind as you belt it out.

So make sure to play not just the music—but the right music—in your head as you write down the lyrics.

The web makes it easy to find the lyrics of most songs. Just go to any search engine and type "the name of the musician/band" + lyrics + "name of the song," and dozens of websites will pop up with the lyrics ready for you to write up. Or you can just pop in the music and write down the lyrics as the song plays.

> *With some songs, I must admit, it's not quite that easy. Two of my favorite songs are sung in languages I do not know. One of the songs is from a tape given to me years back by an ex-girlfriend of some musicians she met while living in another country. It was recorded in a living room. It's an original piece with some of the most beautiful, haunting melodious singing I have ever heard. The other song is from a movie sound track, just a gorgeous song that rattles and shakes even the guarded fibers of practiced poker-faced emotions. Part of me is afraid to get the lyrics translated—I don't want the actual words to alter what these songs mean to me. But there's also a good chance that these songs will have even more impact once the lyrics are revealed to me. Being a word man, it's a chance worth taking.*

⑥ VARIATIONS ON PROJECT #14

1. Write down all your favorite quotes—the ones on or under the magnets stuck to your fridge, featured on the cards you always buy to mail to friends, or written on the first page of your journal. Why do these quotes impact you? Why have they become personal anthems? What larger body of work do they come from, and have you even read the whole thing? Write it all down.

2. Write down all your favorite movie lines. How old were you when you saw each movie for the first time? Who were you with? Is the movie theater you saw it in even there anymore? Which line made you laugh the loudest and longest? Which line can still send a chill up your spine?

3. Write down your favorite passages from your favorite books.

4. Write down all the major world events—front page, bold headline stories—that stick out crystal clear in your mind—all your "Where were you when Kennedy was shot?" moments.

5. Write down all those memories that feel like they just happened yesterday.

6. Write down, from memory, descriptions of the art pieces that you've seen or experienced that have had a lasting impact. After you're done, find images of the art and place them on or near the corresponding text. Make a little book out of it, an exhibit catalog of the museum in your mind.

SET UP AN ART GALLERY in your apartment/house.

What is it with that picture of the woman with her legs hoisted up on her dresser, sexily staring into the mirror while putting on lipstick, and the man slyly sitting back

PROJECT

15

in that chair, gazing longingly? Or how about the scene of the couple wrapped up in each other's arms and passionately kissing on a crowded street? Sure, great photos, but it seems like everyone has them hanging on their walls (especially in dorm rooms).

It's time to take down the mass-produced posters. And yes, that includes your Matisse and Picasso poster prints.

Seek out original art, and buy it. There is original art available at whatever price level you can afford. Or go buy some paint, brushes, and some stretched canvases, and make your own paintings. Have a party and invite your guests to create a collaborative painting on a really big canvas. Frame some of your many photographs, or go out and take new photos with the intention of framing them. Build an installation in the corner of your living room. Make a sculpture out of broken coffee cups, empty wine bottles, or the scrap wood piled up behind the garage.

Put the art all over the house, of course, but designate one room, or one corner of a room, as the gallery. You don't have to put up little cards with the name of the piece and the artist's name, but you can definitely throw an opening party.

MAKE THE PERFECT MARGARITA. Then drink one, two, three, or more.

Oh yes, lots of tests must be done. Second, third, and fourth opinions will be necessary, so invite over your crew. Perfect for a hot, lazy Sunday afternoon, or after

one of those long days at work, the type where a broken down copy machine leaves you mumbling curses and thinking about jumping through the window and ending it all as you make your way to the opposite side of the office to the other copier, which will no doubt be involved in a one thousand–sheet multisort-and-staple job.

There are many recipe variations for the perfect margarita, so diligent research and taste-testing is required: study your drinking guides and cookbooks, surf the web, ask the bartender at your favorite bar for advice, and, most of all, consult your friends for details on their special, one-of-a-kind concoctions. Some notes:

You don't want to use tequila that costs over $50 a bottle in something you'll be adding all kinds of sweet flavorings to, but using the really cheap stuff is a surefire way to keep your margaritas sub-par. Just be sure to use 100 percent agave tequila. Second, forget the frozen limeade or store-bought margarita mix—you definitely want to use fresh lime and lemon juice. Last, margaritas are best when they're really strong but not too sweet, as are so many things that really matter in terms of the good things in life.

Document where you find your freedom.

WAKE UP AT 5 A.M.

Usually, it's about catching a plane.

But do it just to take advantage of the quiet, early-morning hours. Take a walk. Go for a run. Read the paper, leisurely. Work on your novel. Read a novel. Write

a note to a friend. Write a long, long entry in your journal. Make a huge breakfast. Just sit there, drink coffee, and watch the sun come up.

What's your life expectancy?

THE NEXT TIME you get some bad news, or your wife/husband/girlfriend/boyfriend/best friend gets some bad news, pop open a bottle of champagne.

Don't just go home and flip on the television, barely eat whatever happens to be in the fridge, and sit through

18

whatever crap TV happens to be on the tube. Or if a person close to you tells you he/she's just gotten some bad news, take it upon yourself to make sure that person doesn't just sit on the sofa in front of the television all night and mope.

This isn't a variation on going to a bar and getting smashed-up drunk, drowning your sorrows in beer after beer. Champagne is for celebrations—weddings, championships, election victories, job promotions, anniversaries. But at the same time, why does champagne have to be all about the good times?

Pick up a bottle of champagne, get it where it needs to be, and pop the cork. Pour the glasses and make a toast: "Shit happens" or, "It's always something." Then drink it down. Because it's always, always something.

WRITE DOWN THE STORY of the best night of your life. That's a tall order, something that sounds good on paper, but isn't really realistic—a million times harder than naming your favorite song or movie. So, alright, maybe this should be "Write down the stories of

the most memorable nights in your life." There are the easy ones, the landmark events: the night you lost your virginity, the night you got married (hopefully that's not the same night). But I'm thinking more along the lines of past events that aren't so easily identified, the ones that might take some insignificant scene or obscure reference to bring the event back from the recesses of your memory, but once the memory is triggered, the whole event can play itself out in your mind like it happened just yesterday. The kind of event where the layers of significance are just laid bare and, without words, with just

Plan a picnic for the first day it hits eighty degrees.

a feeling, you can fully understand how the event impacted the foundation of your character.

It was Spring Week during my sophomore year in high school. That's the week that has all kinds of events—rallies, competitions between the classes, a movie night—and then culminates with a big carnival and concert on Friday. But what it's really all about is drinking and smoking pot. During lunch breaks, we were going to somebody's house and raiding their parents' liquor cabinet. At night, we were hanging out—in school yards or baseball diamonds or wherever we could mill about and not get caught—and doing more of the same.

So by Thursday, though we were having fun, the hanging out started to get a little old. We were restless. We wanted action. So around midnight, about fifteen of us headed over to the school.

We weren't quite delinquent enough to spray-paint graffiti all over the school, but that's the kind of thing we wanted to do. Toilet-papering the trees, well, of course that came up, but that's old hat. We wanted to do something different.

And then it came to us. We were going to move all the school's bike racks. And by God, for the next four hours, we moved every single bike rack from the bike rack areas. We put bike racks on rooftops, in the middle of the football field, in front of classroom doors, in front of the administration building, in trees—yes, in trees. We hoisted, carried, pushed, threw, and towed bike racks until no bike racks were left to displace. We were on a mission.

The whole time, we were just beside ourselves with outright joy. We thought we were really sticking it to the administration, and that we would be the talk of the school. We were giving each other high-fives and laughing and feeling like the most powerful people in the world, that we could do anything. One guy kept screaming, "We got the bug . . .we got the bug," referring to the spring fever bug, of course. All night long, "We got the bug."

The next day, I showed up to school expecting there to be all kinds of talk about the bike racks. But nothing seemed different. People were just walking to class, like they normally do.

Of course the maintenance crew gets to the school much earlier than the students. By the time we showed up, most of the bike racks had been put back. There were still some displaced bike racks here and there, but you wouldn't have even taken a second look unless you had been involved in the effort to move them. The only people who had been affected were the people who had to move them back—the maintenance crew. No one else noticed a thing. So there was no fame, no glory, just disappointment and . . . guilt. But damn, we did have the bug.

5 VARIATIONS ON PROJECT #19

1. Write down the story of the night that could have been, but wasn't, the best night of your life.

2. Write down the story of the worst night of your life.

3. Write down what you think of as a perfect morning. Where are you? What time do you get up? Who's there with you? What kind of silence is in the room? What's for breakfast? What does the light hit first when you throw open the curtains? How long do you lay there without moving a muscle? How long does the first stretch last? What's the first thing you see when you open your eyes?

4. Write down the story of a night that just flew by—how before you knew it, you were watching the sun come up.

5. Write down how you can make the day last forever.

WRITE SOME LETTERS. Then, go to the library and place the letters in some books, preferably ones you think aren't checked out very often. Or place them in books at a used bookstore, preferably books that might not be purchased for a long time. The letters can be

PROJECT **20**

about anything, to anyone, but keep them anonymous, untraceable. First names only, or no names at all. The people who find the letters get to imagine the lives outside of the words on paper.

TAKE ONE PICTURE every day for a month.

Get a new roll of film with thirty-six exposures and load it into your camera. Then, either take a picture of the same scene every day at the same time for thirty days, or just go about your day and make sure to take

21

one picture each day for a month. You could also take a picture of yourself, or someone you are close to, for thirty days straight.

At the end of the month, get the film developed, put the pictures in chronological order, and place them in some kind of a book or photo album. Or make a poster out of them, put them in a special box, or post them on a bulletin board.

In the movie Smoke, *the shopkeeper (Harvey Keitel) of the smoke shop takes a picture of the street scene from the doorway of his shop every day at the same time. He's done it for years, and keeps all the photographs in photo albums. He's showing one of the photo albums to a regular customer (William Hurt), and the customer is just hurriedly looking through the album. The shop-keeper tells him to slow down, that he's missing the point. The customer then starts to look at the photos more carefully and finds one in which his wife, who is now dead, is captured simply walking down the street.*

WRITE IN THE MARGINS of your books. Underline your favorite passages. Then, make sure to donate the books, or sell them to a used bookstore, to put them back into circulation.

Remember in the movie Heathers, *the big deal that is made out of the single word* Eskimo,* *which is underlined in the copy of* Moby-Dick?

---

* Spelled *Esquimaux* in Herman Melville's *Moby-Dick*.

DOCUMENT THE LIFE OF THE PARTY.

Take a picture of the main room before anyone arrives, another when the party is in full swing, and then another after everyone has left. Frame the three photographs in sequence.

PROJECT

23

JEFFREY YAMAGUCHI

STUDY THE LIFE and life's work of an artist.

Go to a museum. Look at the Picassos and the Dalis (pieces by these artists seem to be in *every* museum), of course, but make a real effort to seek out works of art by artists you've never heard of, the artists without the big

names. Read the white placards, which are always so elegantly written and so perfectly concise, providing just the right amount of information as you stand before and view the original works.

But the information gathering shouldn't end there. Though the story is the art, there's always more to the story. Curate your own retrospective of an artist using the web, books, museums, museum bookstores, and even postcards. An author may only write one book, a filmmaker may make just a few films, but an artist usually builds an expansive body of work. A single painting—or a few paintings—in a museum is just a starting-off point.

I'm a sucker. I admit that I went through an Andy Warhol phase. I sought out his art in every museum I visited, even read his books and watched his movies. I also read books and watched film documentaries about him. I didn't just appreciate his art— I wanted to live his life as an artist, with my very own Factory. I also went through a Dali phase. Again, I sought out the art, read the books, and claimed to "get" Un Chien Andalou. I'm such a poser that right after I saw the movie Surviving Picasso, I started painting. Give me a break.

But regardless of my cliched responses to these artists, I learned a great deal about their lives and their art. And I got inspired . . . to create, to make things, even to paint, despite a total lack of both talent and technique. These days I make an effort to discover and learn about lesser-known artists whose names I have never heard of and whose work I have never seen before. But I still entertain dreams of one day having my own Warhol-like Factory, silver balloons and all.

WAKE UP. CALL IN SICK. Use the day to do that thing you've been meaning to do.

Saturdays are for laundry, errands, get-togethers, shows, all-day events, day trips, going out. Sundays are for waking up late, going to brunch or church or both,

25

mowing/sweeping/vacuuming, matinees, picnics in the park, afternoon beers, watching the game, long-distance phone calls, going to the grocery store, big dinners. And, of course, weekdays are usually for work. Sick days are yours to take, yours to make. Use them wisely.

FIRST, WRITE DOWN your thoughts about your job—what you like about it, what you hate about it, where you think it's going, and how it relates to what you truly want to accomplish with your life.

Then, watch the movie *Ikiru*, by Akira Kurosawa.

Right after the movie, write down your thoughts about your job—what you like about it, what you hate about it, where you think it's going, and how it relates to what you truly want to accomplish with your life.

6 VARIATIONS ON PROJECT #26

1. Right when you arrive at work and sit down at your desk, immediately after flipping on your computer but before you start checking your email (or the online version of the newspaper you read), write down what you have to get done that day. Detail all the calls you have to make and the numbers you have to crunch and the emails you have to write and reply to, as well as any reports you have to turn in or any other deadlines you have to meet. After you are done writing up this list, write down how you feel about your job.

2. Take a picture of yourself first thing when you wake up Monday morning. Take another picture just before you leave for work, and another just after you sit down at your desk. Take pictures of yourself throughout the day at specific times. Be sure to take one just before you leave work for the day. Repeat the picture-taking for each day of the week—Monday through Friday. After you get them developed, organize in sequence, and then flip through the pictures. What do you see?

3. Open up the résumé that is saved on your computer at work (you know you have it stored in a discreetly named file, somewhere on your hard drive). While you're on the clock, add in a new job at the end of your résumé. This is the job you want but do not have. What is the title? What are your responsibilities? What have you accomplished? After you've written out how your ideal job will look on your résumé, take some additional company time and realistically assess what it will take to land that job. Write out the steps. Before you go home that day, take step 1. If you've still got any time left, write your letter of resignation. Date the letter. You just set your deadline.

4. There's no way around it—there are only twenty-four hours in a day. If you sleep for seven of those hours, that leaves you seventeen waking hours. Subtract a half hour to get ready in the morning (people with kids are laughing their asses off at this estimate), a half hour to get to work, and another half hour to get back home at the end of the day. That leaves fifteen-and-a-half hours. You spend maybe an hour and a half on meals (the people with kids are laughing even harder now), an hour on errands and miscellaneous things on your to-do list, and you watch a couple hours of television a day. Now we're down to eleven hours. Of those eleven hours, most likely the bulk of that time, if not all of it, is spent on the job.

So the place you spend the most time on any given day is at work. Map out your own daily timetable, with your own accounting of how your hours are used up. Everyone's timetable will be different, but we're all up against the limit of twenty-four hours. What comes to mind as you look at your daily schedule? How does it make you view your job when you realize such a huge portion of your life is spent at work? Write it all down.

5. List and describe all the jobs you've ever mentioned when someone has asked, "What do you want to be when you grow up?" Remember that even after you've "grown up," people have still asked you that question. At the end of the list, write down your current job. How does it fit in?

6. "I don't need a new job. I need a new career." It's a comment I make regularly—too often, in fact. But it's an honest assessment, and when I break it down, it means the following: that I don't like my current job, that finding a new job isn't necessarily going to make me feel better, that I feel trapped, that I'm scared about where I am on my career path, and that disrupting my current career trajectory to break into a new field isn't really an option—or at least it doesn't feel like a real possibility. That I feel, deep down, where it counts, like I'm not accomplishing anything worthwhile, and my life is just passing me by. I don't just make this comment after the bad days. It's in the quiet moments, when I'm out for a drink with a close friend and we've had more than a few, when I'm talking to no one and just staring into my computer screen, after the lights have just been turned out and I know that I'm not going to be able to fall asleep.

What's the one thing you always say about your job situation? Break it down.

TAKE A PICTURE of a kid you know well: your niece, nephew, younger sister or brother.

Then, make a postcard out of the picture and mail it to the kid.

27

My photography teacher was reviewing some of my photographs and he stopped at one that I had taken of my little sister. "You should print this out a little smaller, put a stamp on the back and then mail it to her," he said. "Kids like getting stuff in the mail, and they're just blown away when they see a picture of them-selves arrive like that . . . They feel famous, in a kid sort of way."

THE NEXT TIME IT RAINS, go collect all the discarded broken umbrellas. They litter the slicked-down streets and sidewalks, all snapped spokes and sagging shields, left exposed to the elements from which they

28 PROJECT

used to provide shelter. Give them a proper burial. Make sure to document your efforts.

GET A REGULAR-SIZED ENVELOPE. Address it to someone special. Then, stuff it with as many things as you can: a letter, photographs, torn out magazine articles or newspaper clippings, photocopies of poems, a short story or passages from a novel, recipes, artwork,

29

poems or stories you've written . . . Anything that can be folded up and put in the envelope. Make sure to stuff it so full that you need to use tape to keep it sealed. This envelope should have serious heft. Once it's sealed, get the proper postage put on it (definitely use stamps) and mail it off.

List those with whom you've shared body heat.

MAKE YOUR OWN ANTHOLOGY. (Why should Norton have a lock on this?)

It's sort of like a mixed tape, really. And people are always making mixed tapes, for themselves, for new girl-friends or boyfriends, and for friends. Why not do the

PROJECT 30

same with the written word? Spread all your books on the floor and start making a list of your favorite stories, your favorite passages from novels, your favorite poems. Then, in a backpack, load up all the books that contain your selections, get to a copy machine, and make copies. After the copying is done, make a cover. Finally, spiral-bind your collection. Voilà! *Your Anthology, Volume 1,* is complete.

Gather a group to sing "99 Bottles of Beer on the Wall."

PUT NEW PHOTOGRAPHS in all of your picture frames.

31 *

Interview someone who is over 100 years-old.

THE NEXT TIME you go to a party, leave a note for the host.

Say that it was a great party. That everyone was having a good time. That you enjoyed yourself spectacularly. And be sure to relate some details, like bits from overheard conversations, the reaction to a certain groove, wild spec-

PROJECT

32

ulations on who might have hooked up, imagined scenes inspired by real incidents, who left in a huff, and who drank way too much.

If you happen to have a Polaroid camera, bring it along, take some pictures during the party, and leave the images with the note.

A great place to put the note (and photos) is under the host's pillow or on his nightstand, right in front of the alarm clock. That way, after all the guests have left, the music has stopped, and the lights throughout the house have been turned off, the last thing that the host will see before he crashes is your note of appreciation.

Write out your life lesson.

FIND THE FIRST POEM you ever wrote.

Read it over. Try to remember the story of why you wrote it, what inspired you, and who it was for. Write it all down.

Then, write a new poem. Once you're done, date it,

PROJECT

33

and put your first poem and the new one back in the place where you found the first one, so that they can both be rediscovered at some point in the future.

Write the story of the last time your temperature hit 102°.

5 VARIATIONS ON PROJECT #33

1. Find the first story you ever wrote. Give it a good read and spend some time enjoying the memory of how you came up with the idea and put it down on paper. Then, rewrite the story.

2. Find the first letter you got during your high school years. Look up the person who penned the note, and then send a reply. (Enclose a copy of the original letter.)

3. Find your first journal. Sit down and read it all the way through (as painful as that might be), making notes in your current journal along the way. What can you remember like it happened yesterday? What extremely significant event, as covered in one or more entries, is something that you can't, for the life of you, remember at all? What makes you blush, and what brings it all back? What makes you think, "What the hell was I thinking?" What makes you wish you could go back in time and do it all over again? What makes you thank God it's all over? What's it like rediscovering the early discoveries of your life, as written down in your first journal? What lessons have you learned, it seems, over and over again?

4. Find the first pictures you ever took with your very first camera.

5. Find the very first picture ever taken of you with the love of your life.

PHOTOGRAPH YOUR BOOKSHELVES. Then, make a list of every book that's on the shelves, putting a check mark next to the books that you've actually read.

Next, make a list of all the books that aren't on the shelves that you've read over the years. Some you'll have

no problem remembering, others you won't be able to recall. And then make still another list, this one noting all the books you want to read but haven't—yet.

Update frequently, and keep the lists and photographs tucked away in your favorite book.

WRITE DOWN THE STORY of an incident—perhaps *the* incident—in which you're just lucky to be alive to tell the tale.

35

STAY UP ALL NIGHT.

Way, way back in the day, this meant making it through *Saturday Night Live.* Slumber party antics would then ensue—the dope who fell asleep first, well, he got his hand put in warm water, maybe even lifted out into the

backyard if he was a real deep sleeper. I can vividly remember tying a pair of shoes together, and then, in the dark, hurling them up in the air and across the room. "Owwwww," someone would scream. The lights would come on, and the person who got hit would spend the next hour demanding to know who threw the shoes. Eventually, everyone would be blaming everyone else.

Next phase: Someone's parents would go out of town, and the drinking would last all night. You sneak out, you stay out.

In college, we'd regularly pull "all-nighters." How

I spent all those late night hours poring over economic theory, I'll never know.

Soon, Jack Kerouac enters the scene. You read *On the Road*, and the next thing you know, you're drinking bad coffee and writing even worse poetry at a dive diner at 3 A.M.

Think about it—all the shit that can go down in one night. The party of the century. The best talk ever. Sexual reckonings. A painting. A short story. A short film. Old friends, good scotch, and the conversations you never get tired of having. New friends, cheap drinks, and discussions about favorite movies. A long drive through the middle of nowhere, stopping to get a large coffee every time you see a gas station. Pounding grooves that keep your body swaying, going way past the point where your legs feel tired. Talking and talking and just talking with the girl/guy who's going to change your life, for one night, for years, forever. The fight that finally ends it. You lay your cards on the table, over and over again. All this and more can happen in one night.

Just don't fall asleep.

TRACK DOWN A PICTURE of every place you have ever lived.

Not the geographical location, but the physical structure you called home. From the house or apartment you grew up in, to your dorm room freshman year, to

all the apartments in various cities and countries you've lived in over the years (for which you may or may not have actually been on the lease), all the way up to the place you currently live.

Some of the pictures will be from parties that you threw. One will be a picture of the family in front of the house. Another will be an image of the cat sleeping on the bed. One will be of you, standing near the door and dressed to the nines, holding a beer. There may be one of a person you can't even recall knowing, sitting in a chair in your living room. There will surely be one place for which you won't be able to find a single photographic record. One will be a picture of the hallway, probably taken just to use up the last picture on the roll. One will be of you and an ex, just hanging out on a lazy Sunday afternoon, taking pictures of each other because you're still in the phase of being in awe of your mutual attraction for each other. And one will be just of the place, because you are so happy with how it looks and proud to call it yours.

ON ONE OF THOSE rainy days when the season is not quite ready to make its shift into the next, those noticeably different, quirky days that bridge summer to fall, or winter to spring, take a picture outside the one window that you always go to when you just want to stare

outside and feel comforted by the fact that you are on the inside looking out at the whole world. Maybe it's a landscape of backyards, clotheslines and patios, and stacks of leaves. Your front yard and the quiet street in front of your house. A view of the city lit up at night, a sea of yellow cabs down below. The apartment building across the way, where the guy on the fifth floor is just sitting in front of his window, like always.

Write down what you see. What's always there? What changes? How long have you known the view? What do you think about when you look outside?

When do you give 110 percent?

GO SOMEPLACE, ALONE. Once you are there, take a picture of yourself, using your camera's self-timer. Immediately after taking the picture, leave, and never go back to that place again. Ever.

39

13 VARIATIONS ON PROJECT #39

1. Take a picture of yourself using the self-timer. In one year, go back to the same spot and take another picture of yourself. Make it an annual tradition.

2. Call up a friend and tell him to meet you at a specific place, somewhere off the beaten path. Use the self-timer on your camera to capture the meeting.

3. Pick a place, and make an effort to photograph—

one by one—all your friends and family members in this specific place. It could be in front of your home, at your favorite bar, underneath a tree in the park. Make sure to date the photographs. How long does it take you to complete this project? How often do you actually get to see those who are closest to you?

4. Go someplace outside your home. Bring along the tools and materials that will allow you to create something—paintbrushes, paint, and canvas; tape and tape recorder; pen and paper; needles and yarn; hammer, wood, saw, and nails. Lay out the tools and raw materials before you, and use the self-timer to take a picture. Build your creation. Once you are done, take a picture of yourself with your finished project.

5. Head someplace specific at sunrise and take a picture of yourself. Then, go about your day. Just as the sun begins to set, return to the site of the early morning photograph and take another picture of yourself.

6. Begin sending disposable cameras to your friends and family members. Give each person the same instructions: "Please go someplace alone and take one picture of yourself. Once you have taken the picture, immediately leave that place, and never go back. Ever."

7. Go through old photos and stop at the first one of yourself that evokes an unexpected response. Make a point of going back to the place where the photo was taken. Take a picture of yourself in exactly the place where you are positioned in the original photograph.

8. The next time you are out with an old friend, at the first instance in which one of you says, "Remember that time . . .?" immediately suggest that you make your way back to the place of the memorable incident. Once there, document the return with a photograph.

9. Go through your old family photographs and find one connected to a significant story, one that is a connective link in the family's collective memory. Then, seek out the place in the photograph, and take a picture of yourself there. Take note of all that has changed and all that has remained the same.

10. The next time you are feeling really depressed, instead of just sitting there and flipping channels, take a picture of yourself, a close-up of your face. Try to remain expressionless. Then, go to a place that cheers you up: a place with good memories, a place where you can just feel safe and comfortable. The park, maybe. In your garden. The front steps of a museum. Your favorite coffee shop. Once you're at the right place, take a picture of yourself. A close-up. Again, try to remain expressionless.

11. Go someplace that's easy to get to, a place that's part of your daily routine. Map out a schedule with a set time frame that allows you to make a daily visit to this place. During your daily visits, take a picture of yourself and write down your thoughts and feelings right there and then. Stay in the moment and capture the essence of what's going on inside your head. At the end of the established time frame, match up the pictures with the text entries.

12. Take a picture of a place that is one of your regular haunts—a particular lunch table, a park bench where you read, the lawn where you kick back before classes, a café or bar where you hang out, the front steps of your church. Then, go someplace you have never been before, and take a picture. Frame the pictures side by side.

13. Write down your vision of a place that you have never been before. Get as detailed as you can. Circle back and add details to the details. Then circle back again. Once you've fully fleshed out even the tiniest of visual nuances in words, go to the place so alive in your imagination. Once you are there, take a picture.

After some time has passed, but with the place still fresh in your memory, compare and contrast the words that you wrote with the picture that you took.

LIST THE YEARS that you have been alive. Then, in a word, sentence, or short paragraph, write down a significant memory from each year.

For years one through four, maybe even years one through eight, you're going to have to sit down with your

40

parents and tap into their memories. It won't be hard for them to come up with stories. Pull out the photo albums to make sure you've got the right memory for each particular year.

Distinguishing important memories from some years will be easy. The year you lost your virginity. The year you almost died. The year your first serious girlfriend or boyfriend dumped your ass and left you crying on the cold kitchen floor, pleading for just one more chance.

Some years won't be so easy. You may have to make some calls and tap into the memories of friends whom you hung out with during periods of time in which your own memory is kind of hazy. Some years just bleed together. Maybe you can't quite put a finger on year twenty-three, or thirty-four, or fifty-eight. Thankfully, good friends have a way of remembering these years for us.

Other years, your most important memory might simply be a fragmentary piece of a fleeting moment in time, something that does not qualify as one of those significant life milestones, and yet it is without question the most significant memory you've got. The time you closed the door on a house for the last time. A midnight phone call that you didn't answer because you knew who was on the other end of the line. Reading a letter you weren't supposed to know existed. Something someone said to you in one of those late-night conversations that has shaped the way you think and feel to this very day.

This list—in the form of words, sentences, short paragraphs, or a combination of all three—is your life calling.

CREATE SOMETHING during the time when you are doing your laundry. The deal with this project is that you can only work on this project when you are doing laundry. It will be known as your "laundry project."

Some laundry project ideas:

Take photographs of the Laundromat. Take photographs in the area around the Laundromat.

Write stories that are all connected in some way to the chore of doing laundry.

Write erotic stories that all take place in a Laundromat.

Write letters to a friend. (Laundry trip 1, Oct 11, 2005; Laundry trip 2, November 1, 2005; Laundry trip 3, November 17, 2005; etc.)

I have to do my laundry at a Laundromat. Since I hate the weekend crowds—fighting for dryers and hoping the kids running around don't spill their canned soda (usually some bright-colored, orange-flavored drink) all over my freshly cleaned clothes—I wake up early on a weekday and do my laundry then, when the place is empty and I have my pick of dryers. I have to get there by 6 A.M. so that I can still make it to work on time. Especially in the dead of winter, getting up that early is rough going. But a total lack of clean underwear or socks, not to mention a giant pile of dirty clothes, usually forces the issue. It just gets to the point where the laundry has to get done.

Once at the Laundromat, I usually just sit there bleary-eyed and tired, and zone out as I watch my clothes get soaped up and make their way through the various wash cycles. Same thing in front of the dryer. I watch the clothes tumble dry and act as if my staring will make the time left on the minutes display dwindle faster.

Of course I bring reading material. Usually the paper. Maybe I'll get through the gossip column, but mostly I just flip through the pages. Sometimes I pull out some paper and make a to-do list for myself, things that I have to get done once I get to work.

It's so quiet in there, just the meditative hum of the machinery. No one around to bug me. It's too early to make phone calls, and certainly no one is going to be calling me at that time in the morning. I've got a seat, as well as empty seats to the left and right of me. It's the perfect place to get some writing done. Why do I just sit there and do nothing?

(Written on July 2, 2003, while doing laundry.)

TAKE SOME CHOPSTICKS from your kitchen drawer (the one where all the take-out chopsticks get thrown), and, along with $25 cash and a take-out Chinese food menu, seal them up in an envelope. Mail off the envelope to one of your currently unemployed friends,

PROJECT 42

your college-aged kid brother or sister, or a person you know who is financially strapped at the moment.

Keep it anonymous. Do not hand-write the mailing address or enclose a note. Include the take-out Chinese food menu regardless of the person's geographical location; you want to be sure that the person you mail the envelope to gets the right message and orders up some good take-out.

MAKE A CAKE. A BIG ONE. Write something obscure on the top of it:

"How about 1972?"
"He just wouldn't SHUT UP!"

43

"Texas, here we come!"
"Tuesday is the day to roll the dice."
"Here's to more closet space!"
"Cubicle 404, YES!"

Then, place the cake in your office's kitchen area or break room. Put paper plates and plastic forks next to it, and make sure to cut out a slice, so people know that it's okay to eat. Don't let anybody see you bring in the cake.

RECORD THE NUANCES of one of your regular ol' days.

At the end of any given day, when you're just about to hit the point when you need to climb into bed to crash, sit down at your kitchen table with a tape recorder,

push the RECORD button, and start talking about your day. Begin with the moment you got up, and take yourself all the way to the point where you are recording yourself at the kitchen table. Mention names, places, things that you saw on the way to work, what you got done, what you didn't get done, phone calls that you made and received, emails that you sent, overheard conversations, elevator banter, what you ate, the funny thing that happened on the way to that meeting. After you're done talking, hit STOP, eject the tape, write down *My Day* and the date on the tape, and file the tape away.

WRITE A ONE-MINUTE AUTOBIOGRAPHY.

Don't necessarily start at the beginning, and don't worry about the ending. Indeed, do not let any kind of chronological order hinder your effort. A good place to start is the first thing that comes to mind. Once you

PROJECT

start writing, other memories will pop into your head. Go with them. The interruptions enhance the flow.

Once the minute is up, read over what you have written, and then immediately repeat the exercise. Keep going for as long as you can.

4 VARIATIONS ON PROJECT #45

(Repeat each variation after each minute is up for as long as you can.)

1. Write for one minute about the biggest mistake you've ever made.

2. Write for one minute about the person who means the most to you.

3. Write for one minute about your most vivid memory.

4. Write for one minute about what you want to do with your life.

BEFORE YOUR NEXT HAIRCUT, take a headshot photo. Immediately after your haircut, take another headshot photo. Proceed to take the same photo every day until your next haircut. Once the cycle is complete, place the photos in a photo album that flips easily. Watch your hair grow.

PROJECT

46

5 VARIATIONS ON PROJECT #46

1. Take pictures of yourself before and after your workouts, over a set period of time. Ideally, you'll initiate this series of photos just as you begin a new, regimented exercise routine, or perhaps just as you start an exercise routine for the very first time in your life. Focus the lens on whatever you are focusing on in the workouts.

2. Take pictures of you and your significant other before and after significant pleasure. (Get your mind out of the gutter. Or get your mind into the gutter. Up to you.)

3. Take a picture of yourself (or you and your spouse/ significant other, or the whole family) before you leave for vacation, and then right when you walk in the door upon your return. Or take a photo on each day of your vacation, making sure to also get a shot before you depart to your destination, and one immediately after you return home.

4. Take pictures of yourself as you go through the process of trying to quit smoking. Every time you want to reach for a cigarette, take a picture of yourself instead.

5. Take a picture of yourself in the same spot, a place where you can really get a sense of the surroundings, on the official start of each season—winter, spring, summer, and fall.

PROJECT

47

Most everyone else had been caught, so the game was clearly coming to an end. Looking for people is never as fun as hiding from them. I had managed to stay safe, despite several close calls in open space. I had run across the lawn, thinking no one was around, but a couple of the girls had been resting, just laying on their backs and staring up into the star-filled night sky. At about the halfway point, one of them screamed, "There he is!"

Shit. *It's the only word that comes to mind when you're playing ditch and you get spotted, but still have enough distance between you and those who are trying to hunt you down to maybe, possibly, hopefully, make it to safety.*

I picked up the pace and headed for the deepest, darkest patch of bushes. Are my feet making all that noise, or are they right behind me? Don't look back. Just get to the bushes and dive.

Once you hit the ground, you push out whatever branches are keeping you from maneuvering, and you start crawling. It's okay to make some noise, right at the beginning—the pursuers have seen exactly where you jumped in—but stealth mode goes into effect the second you start heading in a new direction. Otherwise, you just get trapped, tagged, and laughed at the second you peek your head out of the bushes. All the scratches on your skin and the dirt on your clothes were for nothing. I listened for footsteps. Nothing. I don't think the girls were even looking. They probably didn't even get up. That's how they're having fun now—watching the idiots still hiding, ducking for cover even though no one is going to bother to really chase them.

The deep-cover mind-set is hard to shake, however. If you walk out to ask if the game is over, well, then, it's definitely over. So you just stay patient, listen, and pretend like someone is quite possibly stalking you, waiting for you to take just one more step, right into their trap. Tag. You're out.

Still, you can only bide your time for so long. You wait and wait, but still hear nothing, and at some point you've got to walk out there and find out what the hell is going on. This is the most stressful moment. To break cover or to hold out. Making the decision to go from one to the other is the life-or-death decision in ditch.

. . .

I made my way out of the bushes, into the center. This area was shielded from the park's lighting, but the full moon graced an illuminating glow over the area.

He was standing so still, I wouldn't have even noticed him had he not spoken. "Jeff?"

It was T. The way he whispered, I knew he was still in the game. My God, we were both still alive.

I ran toward T. and he ran toward me, slowly at first, and then with the speed of a full-on sprint. We dove into each other's arms. There was something manic in the way we were celebrating, as if getting caught might have meant more than the end of a game. We were laughing loudly enough to give up our position. But no one came. They had all turned in and were probably having a chuckle about how we were still out there, hiding. But we had the last laugh. We definitely had the last laugh.

8 VARIATIONS ON PROJECT #47

1. Remember all the places you used to go to read your books—when you were a kid, while you were in college, on Sunday mornings, after a long day at work. Try to remember which books you read in these various places.

2. Remember the place you used to go to be alone.

3. Remember the spots you used to hang out at during lunch.

4. Remember the places you used to park the car and make out.

5. Remember all the places where you've had breakdowns—mental or otherwise.

6. Remember the places where, after it got dark, you felt heart-thumping, "What was that noise?" or "Who's there?" fear.

7. Remember all the places where you've seen falling stars.

8. Remember all the trees you've climbed up as far as you could climb.

MAKE A BOX WITH SOMEONE SPECIAL in mind, something that will slide easily under the bed or fit in an underwear drawer. Then, place a single letter in the box, and mail it off to that special someone (even

48

if you share a home). In the letter, make sure to mention that you plan, in the years to come, to fill the box with letters.

DURING THE NEXT SUMMER rainstorm, walk outside to a place without shelter and immediately take a picture of yourself (and whomever else you can convince to join you). Keep standing in the rain until you

PROJECT

49

are soaked to the bone. Once you are thoroughly and completely drenched, take another photo.

GO TO THE LIBRARY. Find your favorite writer's books. Then, see which writer comes next on the shelf. Someone you've never heard of before? Good. Check out the works of this newly discovered writer and start reading.

50

ASK YOUR GRANDPARENTS to tell you some stories. Make sure to document these stories, either in writing, on tape, or on video.

PROJECT
51

"I got a call from the school. They said, 'Come in right away.' So I left work and headed over there. I was worried that your dad had gotten hurt.

"But when I got there, your dad was just sitting on the bench right outside the principal's office. He didn't say a word. He seemed very calm.

"The principal waved me in and closed the door. He thanked me for coming in on such short notice and then told me that your dad had threatened him.

"I asked, 'What happened?'

"The principal explained that he had caught one of your

dad's friends misbehaving. "I had taken hold of the boy's arm, to escort him to the office, when your son stepped in front of me and said, 'Take your hands off him.'"

"I just nodded.

"The principal then said, 'It was quite inappropriate and frightening to be spoken to in that manner.'

"I nodded again, and told him, 'Okay, I will deal with this.' I thanked the principal for his concern, but I didn't apologize.

"I walked out of the office and your dad followed me to the car. I didn't even say anything to him. He wasn't in trouble with me, see, because I knew your dad. I knew that was just his way."

MAKE A LIST OF THE PROJECTS that you want to complete. Write it in your journal, and maybe post the list on your refrigerator as well. Then, start doing the projects on your list.

PROJECT

52

We all have stories. Some make us laugh, others can make us sad. Some we tell over and over again, and others we don't tell anyone at all. Some are intended for just one person, others are for dinner parties. There's a never-ending supply. You go through the day, just an ordinary day, and you've got stories to tell. And there are, of course, all the major events, the big surprises, the tragedies, the best days ever, the triumphs that create the marking points in the times of our lives, the way we remember what happened and when, the things that shape us and explain the current state of what we are doing in the here and now.

It's so important to write these stories down. Just as easy as it is to tell a story, say, in the car on the way to a restaurant, or sitting around the living room with friends in the cool, quiet hours well past midnight, or in bed after the lights have been turned out—putting words down on paper is a simple exercise that we're all clearly capable of and equipped to execute. You just have to sit down with a pen and paper, or in front of the computer, and let the words flow.

Certainly it's about preserving the stories. If not committed to paper, we might not remember even those events that at the time of their happening seemed like something we would never, ever forget. But mostly it's about the smaller details. They definitely have a way of slipping from memory . . . and the fewer details you have, the harder it becomes to conjure the story, bring it back to life, and understand what meaning it has in the bigger scheme of your current world.

But it's also about sorting out your feelings; getting some clarity on what exactly happened; what is making you so angry, happy, or sad; how it impacts your relationships; how you are making your way through the day-to-day; and what it might mean for the long haul. You may not realize how much a particular event or person or place means to you until you've written about it. It may help you draw conclusions—why you are right, or figuring out why you are wrong. Perhaps it will help you make a big decision, or keep you moving forward despite setbacks and anticipated difficulties ahead. Having to collect your thoughts to create a coherent, written account may lead you to discover new or different reasons as to why the elements that make up your story mean something to you.

Putting the words down on paper has a way of revealing the truth. It might include all those things you don't reveal when you are relating the story out loud, even if you are telling your closest friend in one of those never-ending, late-night conversations. The written words, as they come from your mind and heart, using the mechanics of your body to spell them all out, may very well spring forth the hidden, sometimes hard-to-grasp truth of how you feel deep inside.

Or you just might find a way to make funny stories even more hilarious. It doesn't have to be so serious. The main thing is to make a habit out of documenting your stories. Don't use the excuse that you don't have time. Don't worry that you don't have the writing skills of F. Scott Fitzgerald. Don't worry that your writing isn't going to get published and become a bestseller. Sit down, shut up, and start writing. It's that simple.

What you do with these writings is wide open—the project possibilities are as endless as the stories you have within you.

You could simply fill up a personal journal with your stories, or create a special-edition bound book to give to friends and family members. You could design a broadside and post it around your neighborhood, or print them out on nice paper and seal them in fancy envelopes to mail off or slip into used books for sale at a thrift shop. You could begin a story exchange, sending off your stories with the request to return the favor in kind. You could design a website based around your stories, making them available worldwide, or you could stick them in a handcrafted box to present to your significant other.

Of course, all of these projects begin with you sitting down and actually writing a story. And it really is as easy as sitting down, with pen and paper in hand, or in front of a computer, and placing one word after another. You've got an endless reserve of stories worth getting down on paper, and each passing day offers up new ones to chronicle. The trick is to actually begin the story. Don't let potential blocks—such as insecurity about your writing ability, indecision about which of your stories is worth putting down on paper, or the fear that your story won't be any good—prevent you from seeing it as the simple exercise that it most definitely is. Fears be damned! Just get your fingers on the keypad and start pounding away. All the obstacles will fade deeper and deeper into the background with each word that you type.

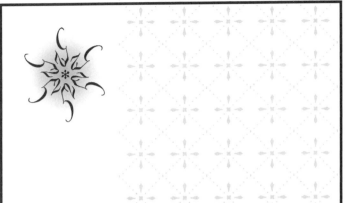

CAPTURING THE MOMENTS

$\mathbb{J}$ust a click on the button, and that moment in time, as seen through the viewfinder of your camera, is preserved in the form of a photograph. Something that happened, and will never happen again, has been documented. The setting and the scene, the expressions and emotions, they're all anchored into the permanent and perfect stillness of a single image. The moment is captured.

It's weird to think that we only have so many moments in the span of our life. Once they happen, they are gone, forever. While you certainly can't photograph every single moment, the pictures that you do take create a unique way to chronicle the people, places, and things that fill up your life.

In these photos are glimpses, big and small, of our actions and accomplishments, the lives of our friends and family, the arcs of relationships, of cities visited and countries toured, of the times that we live in. And also images of the kids. Always pictures of the kids doing one of their many cute things. (No kids? Then it's pictures of the pets.)

Just as important as it is to get that picture of your son receiving his diploma, or the moment in the wedding ceremony when the bride and groom seal the deal with a kiss, when you cross the finish line, or gather everybody up for the big group photo, so too must the smaller, innocuous moments be captured. Photos taken around the house on a lazy Sunday afternoon, getting ready to go out to dinner for no particular reason other than to grab something to eat, the way the house looks after all the guests leave. The quiet moments, the going-through of everyday motions, the moments when no one is posing—pictures that freeze-frame those seemingly unremarkable incidents of day-to-day life—often reveal more about who we are and the way we live than photographs of the landmark moments at big life events.

It all starts with taking pictures, of course. If you don't take them, there are no photos to document any of your moments at all. The general rule of thumb, then, should be to keep a camera on you at all times. Don't just throw it in your bag when you go on vacation, or only break it out at weddings or birthday parties. New Year's Eve certainly isn't the only time you should try to photograph celebratory festivities.

The more photographs you take, the better you'll get at capturing these moments. It will become instinctual. Your visualization of the scene—all the movement and facial expressions, heads being thrown back with laughter, arms flailing about during a particularly animated discussion—will feed a lightning-speed impulse to click your finger on the button. Before you even have time to think about whether or not you've got the shot, your photograph will already have locked down the perfect moment in a permanent record.

Your photographs may exhibit the fine grains of perfect exposure and the balance of exquisite lighting, or the flash may have turned your subject's eyes red; maybe everything is off center and certain elements have been awkwardly cropped. Regardless, whether the quality is professional grade or point-and-shoot simple, there's a story—and value—in every photograph.

The person who is always taking photos —now that's the person we should aspire to be.

So here's to the guy who's desperately trying to avoid having to go out on the dance floor, so instead, he becomes the event photographer, capturing the laughter and the grooves and the spills, from beginning to the bitter end.

Here's to the guy who finally wears his girlfriend

down (who in the beginning only allowed the camera to be out of its case when she was done up and posing) and finally gets to take pictures of her whenever and however he wants, candid and natural, like right when she wakes up in the morning after one of those long nights that involved heavy drinking and questions about not only when, but how, you got home.

Here's to the young girl who discovers the life and work of Berenice Abbott or Tina Modotti, and begins to carry a camera around with her wherever she goes.

Here's to the crazy father who cajoles everyone to get together in the living room for a photo session—who disregards the moans and groans and complaints, isn't afraid to say, "One more picture, just one more picture," about five or six times, and works his magic until he knows his magic has captured the perfect family portrait (with both dogs sitting down and looking straight ahead, of course).

Of course, taking photos is just the first part of the project-making process. Now that you have the photographs in hand, you can use them to embark on any number of creative projects. It goes without saying that photos are meant to be seen and shared.

Photo-based projects can be as simple as mailing off a packet of photos with a story enclosed, or as elaborate as mounting photos in a handmade book filled with journal entries and other mementos. You can enlarge a photo as big as the largest wall in your house, or turn it into a postcard. Publish an online slideshow. Mount a photograph in a frame that you've designed and decorated, or seal it on the inside of an antique glass jar. Photo albums are nice, a necessity really, but don't limit yourself to just putting your photos in an album.

There is always the danger of being struck by the "Storage Bin Syndrome," a rather common affliction in which packet after packet of photos gets thrown into one of those file-folder storage bins. The cure is easy. Simply dig into that box, seek out photos that feature memorable moments and close friends, and mail them off to the people in the images. Once you begin rooting around in that box, taking a good look at what's inside of it, the impulse to do something with all those captured moments will take hold of you.

That is an impulse that should be multiplied, emulated, and celebrated.

So here's to the good buddy who takes photos at all the events, and actually sends them around to everyone like he says he's going to.

Here's to the person who cuts mat board herself, and not only fills her own home with framed photographs, but also generously gives them out as gifts to friends and family.

Here's to the friend who makes unique scrapbooks for friends, filled with photographs that celebrate shared adventures and fond memories.

Here's to the person who digs up old photos and mails them off to friends, providing a wallop of memories, and, depending on the hairstyle and attire, one hell of a laugh.

Here's to the mom who keeps all the family pictures —from the soccer team photos to the black-and-whites that belonged to her grandparents—organized, accessible, and safe.

The thing I like to remember about photographs is the answer most people give when they are asked the question, "If your house were burning down, what's the one thing you would try to save (assuming your family members/roommates and pets have already made it to safety)?" Most people say they would grab their photo albums. Makes perfect sense to me. There's a personal history in those photos, a family history, images of people who have passed away, images of youth, of growing up, of the people who have been in our lives, the places we've seen and the things we've accomplished, the homes we have lived in, the way we look when we're all dolled up and dressed to the nines, the way we used to wear our hair all those years ago, the way we laugh, and all the smiles. There are always so many smiles in pictures—the way we look when we're happy. The photos provide connections to the people and stories and histories and the times of our very lives.

The emotions these photographs evoke run the full spectrum, from pit-in-your-stomach sadness to laugh-out-loud happiness. And it's never clear-cut how you will react: The feelings elicited from looking at a particular picture will never fail to surprise. A photo of a dear friend who has passed away may remind you of a story that brings the smile of smiles to your face; a recently taken group photograph of your current crew may provoke a tinge of sadness, perhaps because you sense that the end of an era is upon you, or just the end of something you can't quite put your finger on yet.

Pictures of old girlfriends or boyfriends; vacation shots of the ocean view from your hotel balcony in St. Maarten; a group photo of your pals from college, everyone half falling over and holding up plastic cups; a picture of you and one of your oldest friends, a person you haven't seen in years even though you used to talk two times a day.

These images can bring it all back, a cascade of how you felt all those years ago flash flooding into your emotional state of the moment, the blend of the then and now providing an entirely new reaction.

Taking these photos, and using them as launching pads for projects, or initiating a photo session based on a project idea, taps into the energy and meaningfulness that already exists in a simple, stand-alone photograph. Inventive photographic projects take it all a step further, increasing the value and expressiveness of something that already qualifies as a treasure. Add in your own personal creative mix and see what kind of magic you can develop as you take your captured moments and expand their beauty and meaning, and give even greater strength and power to what it is that they evoke.

PROJECTS:
TO GIVE AND TO GET

If you create a project from scratch—utilizing your skills and smarts and imagination, adding in either blood, sweat, and tears, or a combination of all three—that is something special, outright. But if you do all that with someone special in mind, guiding the construction of your creation and inspiring its uniqueness, then you have really, truly created something special. One of the best reasons to make a project is for the specific purpose of giving it as a gift.

And boy, do we have plenty of opportunities to give

gifts: There are birthdays. The holidays. Weddings. Anniversaries. Housewarming parties. Graduations. Baby showers. Mother's Day. Father's Day. Secretary's Day, and all the rest of the fill-in-the-blank days. The list goes on and on. For each celebration, gathering, commemoration, or party, there is an expectation—a social contract, if you will—that you should arrive at the door bearing a gift. And even though we have all these calendared opportunities to share and give gifts, the best time to give one is when it's totally unexpected.

Unfortunately, there's a culture of consumerism that has programmed each and every one of us into believing that we should not only *buy* the gift, but spend the right amount of money on it. This is so ingrained into our brains that if we don't stick to the program, we feel guilty.

But I say bull. And I think most people would agree with that sentiment.

Making a tailor-made gift—something you've put time, thought, and energy into—is an extremely expressive, generous, and kind thing to do. And it's far more meaningful than any item that could have been purchased in a store.

The homemade gifts can range from the simple to the elaborate. You can easily take a photograph and some nice paper and make a card out of it, putting down your own words to express how you feel. Or you could build something more complex—say, a small wooden box, marking it with engravings or painted images or photographs, and filling it up with poems or stories or bits of your shared history together.

Whatever it is, if it's something that you have created and made with a particular person in mind, there are extra dimensions added to the meaning: a sense of the depth of your friendship; an expansive view of your shared connections and history; a further tightening of the bonds between the two of you.

And if you present this gift out of the blue, not on an event or day that dictates the giving of a present, you are absolutely going to make someone's day. If the person is feeling down, it might just be the thing that lifts her up. If she's already feeling on top of the world, your gift *just because* is going to take her to another planet. The goodwill you've initiated has a way of spilling over. You may just set in motion an expanding cycle of inspirational sharing and kindness.

Of course, you, as the gift giver, also get something out of the deal. In a way, the giving of a gift is a gift to yourself. You get the inspiration, or perhaps the incentive, to create something, a surge of energy by working through the process of creation, and the sense of accomplishment once the project is finished. There's also the exciting buzz of knowing you are going to surprise the receiver with your one-of-a-kind gift. And perhaps most of all, you get to see how the giving of your personalized, unique gift makes your friend (or family member, spouse, or significant other) feel really special. All of this is guaranteed to make you feel darn good, inside and out.

Keep in mind that the giving of your projects as gifts does not have to be confined to significant others, close friends, and family. That's usually what our impulses, or the calendar, dictate, but leaving an artistic footprint for people whom you don't know and will never meet is another meaningful and rewarding way to share your projects. It's as simple as taking one of your projects and letting it loose on the world, with the hope that it finds its way into the field of vision of some random person or group of people. What kind of impact it has you will never really know, but the goal would be the same as if you were giving your project to someone in particular: put a smile on someone's face, lift some spirits, inspire some creativity, and, most of all, ignite a cycle of in-kind project-making and sharing.

The desire to give an object of your creation as a gift is truly one of the best incentives to get going on a project. You've got your own ideas, of course, but you also have the inspiration derived from whomever it is that you want to bestow the gift upon. It's a collusive arrangement between your imagination and what you believe will make your special person (or group or whomever it is that you are going to bestow your gift upon) feel special. You've got to do your best, of course, and you've got a reason to get it done as fast as possible: so you can wrap it up and put it in the hands of the person who inspired it.

✳ What events (that involve close friends or family members) do you have coming up that require the giving of a gift?

✳ Who of your friends or family members—someone who is going through a bit of a rough patch—could use the surprise of an out-of-the-blue gift?

✳ What handmade gifts have you anonymously given to a person? Was it hard keeping the secret?

✳ What personalized gift have you received from a secret admirer who never revealed his or her identity?

✳ What are some of the gifts that have been made for you?

✳ What projects have you made and given away as gifts?

✳ What kind of project, given as a "just because" gift, would make your special someone feel really special?

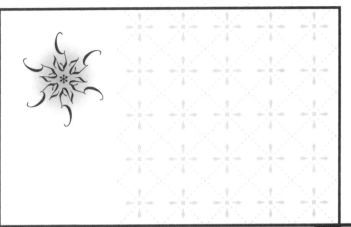

MAKING TIME FOR PROJECT-MAKING

$\mathbb{P}$robably the single biggest obstacle to making projects is the simple excuse of not having enough time. "How do you expect me to make projects? I don't even have time to do all the stuff that I *have* to get done."

It's true. That's one way to look at it. Life gets in the way. Work. Family. Errands. Emergencies. Chores. Someone has to change the litter, make dinner, go to the store to pick up milk. You've got to bring home the bacon, and you've got to fry it up in the pan. Then you have to wash the dishes, and make sandwiches for the next day at lunch, and deal with the complaints about BLT sandwiches, again.

But just like you get all that stuff done—the way you're able to hold down your job and run the household and remember birthdays and plan vacations and call about the newspaper that keeps not getting delivered and bring in your computer to get fixed and get the car an oil change on schedule—you can make time to start and complete projects.

If you really want to.

So that's some simple encouragement to say that it can happen. Easier said than done, you say? It always is. Here, then, are some basic, practical ways to make time for project-making.

✳ Turn off the television.

This is the biggest time magnet of all. You flip it on in the morning to check out the weather, or the traffic, or just to have a little background noise. You turn it on while you cook, or maybe while you eat dinner. You want to catch the news. There's that new show you've been wanting to check out, or you have to see the show you've been a fan of for years. Then there's the news at 11:00, and then *Nightline* or *Leno* or *Letterman*. Is turning off the television the last thing you do before turning out the light and hitting the sack? Hour upon hour, every darn day, your television is burning up your spare moments. Turn it off and keep it off. You just bought yourself some serious project time.

✳ Get rid of cable.

That way, even if you do turn on the television— admittedly, we all need a *little* down time in front of the boob tube—there aren't so many options to suck you in and keep you clicking on the remote. It just makes it easier to shut it off if there are only a few channels to choose from, instead of all those endless choices that cable offers.

✳ Limit the time you surf the web.

I'm all for checking out cool websites. But one click leads to another, and another, and so on and so forth, and when you finally look up from the computer screen, several hours have passed you right on by.

✱ Stop wasting time reading those silly celebrity and fashion magazines.

PR spin, paparazzi shots, and gossip collide in an attempt, I think, to instill the idea that our own normal lives are simply inadequate. Total BS. Do we really need to know the sordid and/or PR-cleansed details about Britney and Ben and Christina and whoever happens to be the reigning throw-away king and queen of reality television this particular week? No, we don't. It's that simple.

✱ Schedule in time for projects.

Sometimes it's as easy as taking a look at the schedule book and marking off time for your project. Just like at the office, when you schedule meetings or training sessions or block off time to complete a major report, if you fill in open slots with your project in mind, you will instill a regimented sensibility into your project-making routine.

✳ Incorporate projects into other things that have to get done.

Instead of just sitting there reading a magazine while you do your laundry at the Laundromat, use that time to make a project. Or instead of just making dinner and serving it up, start documenting the cooking process with your camera, or collecting the recipes you use in a booklet, or recording the stories told during meals at the dinner table—all variations on a sort of culinary diary.

✳ Prioritize project-making just like you prioritize the fact that you have to eat.

Don't simply relegate project-making to the status of a recreational activity you partake in when all of your other tasks have been completed—after the dishes are done, the car is washed, the lawn mowed, all the phone calls returned, and the burned-out bulb in the garage is changed . . . As you can see, the list of things that need to get done never, ever ends. So fit project-making in there, somewhere. There is time for projects, if you make a point of making the time.

✱ **Wake up an hour earlier than you normally do, and work on your projects then.**

Being productive from the moment you roll out of bed is a great way to start out the day.

✱ **Use your lunch break at work for project-making.**

This is either a good solid hour or half hour to do as you please. Instead of surfing the web or reading the paper or your book, or going and spending money that you don't have on $10 lunches with coworkers whom you don't particularly like that much anyway, use this time to work on your projects.

✱ **Do your project on company time.**

Why the heck not? Sneak in some time while you're on the clock. Do you know how many novels, screenplays, plays, and more have been written on the job? This is an old tradition. The main issue here is not to get caught. Don't miss deadlines. Get your "work" work done, of course. But factor in some time here and there to work on your project. You'd be surprised how much time there really is in an eight-hour workday to find time for yourself if you plan things out and work efficiently.

✳ Involve your kids.

Surely between work and managing the household, keeping the kids fed, safe, clean, and occupied is where all your time is spent. So create projects in which your kids are either the subject, helping you out, or collaborating with you.

✳ Incorporate your schoolwork into the projects.

Create projects that are simply extensions of the various homework assignments you have to complete—term papers or research, books that you have to read, words or history lessons that you have to memorize. Building personal projects around schoolwork doesn't just allow you to make projects; it might also make doing the homework seem a bit less painful.

✳ **Change one habit that eats up a consistent amount of your time on a regular basis.**

Stop watching a soap, waking up late, surfing the web for nothing in particular, renting a movie every single night of the week, staying up just to watch the sports recaps of games for which you already know the final score. By taking this one habit out of the equation, you can open up your schedule for more inspiring, productive project-making time.

✳ **Instead of talking and talking _and talking_ about your project idea, just get to work.**

Procrastination is a huge time magnet, and it sucks up a lot of energy. It also breeds negativity, and lets your mind wander into the minefield of dangerous rationales for avoiding the project, such as finding all kinds of excuses as to why you can't get started, or all the materials that you're lacking and don't have access to, or the fear that you won't do a good job. Just shut up and get to work. The momentum you create just by getting started will move you up and over the challenges you might be confronted with as you make your project.

✳ Here's a project:

Make a list of all the stuff you always have to get done, and how long it takes you to do it all. Document your time. Not just your work schedule or your monthly calendar, but how you spend your minutes during the day. How long does all this stuff *really* take? How much time do you spend spinning your own wheels, either sorting out what to do next, worrying about what's not getting done, or fretting that you don't have enough time to make everything happen? Write it all down. Next, write down all the things you want to do: all the things you feel you never have enough time to actually get started on and fully sink yourself into. Once it's all written out, spend some time thinking about how you can strike a better balance between the items on the two lists. Be sure to make the things you want to do a part of what has to get done.

52 RESOURCES

HOPEFULLY THE POINT has been hammered home that inspiration for projects is all around. It can be found just sitting at your desk while staring out the window, on your walk to work, or in the storage bin with all your old photos. A conversation with an old friend. An afternoon wandering the stacks at the library. Researching the creative process of an artist you admire and respect. Discovering the unknown in your city or your family history. Your mind is always turned on, seeing new things, reliving old memories, calculating possibilities, taking inventory of what you have and don't have, dreaming and daydreaming, and a million other things. To get started on a project, all you have to do is grab hold of one of the ideas floating all around you, pull up your sleeves, and get to work.

But of course seeing the projects of others is one way to inspire the creation of your own. Certainly not to copy. There's no fun in emulating or duplicating someone else's creativity, exactly. But feeding off their energy—and expanding your own creative ideas by witnessing and experiencing someone else's amazing work—is an excellent way to fuel your project-making ventures.

Following is a list of fifty-two resources for inspiration. The list includes websites, books, magazines, 'zines, stories, albums, and more. Some of the items provide how-to information, others invite you to participate. A few require you to do some digging. Some showcase artistic achievement, while others encourage you to explore and examine the creative process. Many do all of the above. There are also spaces in which you are prompted to fill in your own sources of inspiration. This list is really about providing jumping-off points. A heads up: Resource #52 is your own personal, unique list of fifty-two resources. Better get started on that now.

1. Crafty resources such as getcrafty.com; *Get Crafty: Hip Home Ec* by Jean Railla / *Stitch 'n Bitch Nation* by Debbie Stoller / *The Starving Artist's Way* by Nava Lubelski / SuperNaturale.com / KnitKnit.net / Craftster.org. These websites and books provide hands-on instruction and insights into the art of craft-making.

2. sh1ft.org. Wide-open photo assignments, with a link to each participant's completed entry.

3. MirrorProject.com. A participatory photographic project of self-reflection.

4. Nervousness.org. Participatory mail art experiments. Learningtoloveyoumore.com—Creative participatory assignments.

5. phototag.org. Photography project in which disposable cameras are released into the world.

6. *ReadyMade Magazine*. Hip, highly creative, how-to projects for the artful, imaginitive do-it-yourselfer.

7. Scrapbooking magazines, such as *Creating Keepsakes, Memory Makers, Paperkuts,* and *Simple Scrapbooks.* These present ideas and features on making memorable projects out of your memories.

8. *Being Antinova* by Eleanor Antin.

9. *Willy Wonka & the Chocolate Factory.* *"We are the music makers, and we are the dreamers of the dream"*—Arthur O'Shaughnessy, in his poem "Ode."

10. *A Technique for Producing Ideas* by James Webb Young. A short, to-the-point book which explores a step-by-step technique for idea creation. Though written with the development of ad copy in mind, the methodology explored in the book works for any type of project.

11. *Working* by Studs Terkel. We spend a great many of our hours on the clock, perhaps more than we devote to anything else in our lifetimes. From the perspecitve of a cross-section of the workplace—farmer to athlete to fireman to stock broker to waiter—this book is a wonderful examination of what working means to us: how it affects our lives and dreams, breaks us down and builds us up, and gives meaning to our day-to-day existence.

12. 52projects.com. (And also, spell it out.)

13. Walt Whitman's *Leaves of Grass*. The poems, yes, but also the story and the scholarship on the numerous volumes of this collection. *Leaves of Grass* evolved over Whitman's entire lifetime. Learning about and reading the full spectrum of the different versions, and not just the last volume, ramps up the roof level on the already incredible experience that is the poetry of *Leaves of Grass*.

14. The Beatles's *Sgt. Pepper's Lonely Hearts Club Band*. Everything from the album cover to the concept of the concept album. And the music, of course.

15. John Coltrane's *A Love Supreme*.

16. "92 Days" in Big Bad Love by Larry Brown.

17. *Remembering Slavery: African Americans Talk About Their Personal Experiences of Slavery and Emancipation,* edited by Ira Berlin, Marc Favreau, and Steven F. Miller / *Manzanar* by John Armor and Peter Wright, featuring photographs by Ansel Adams and commentary by John Hersey / *Hiroshima* by John Hersey.

18. *The Artist's Way* by Julia Cameron.

19. Zinebook.com. Total 'zine resource—how-to articles, interviews with 'zine publishers, 'zine library information, distribution and promotion information, and more. Operated by Chip Rowe.

20. The life and art (or is it the art of the life?) of the enigmatic artist Ray Johnson. See the film *How to Draw a Bunny* by filmmakers John Walter and Andrew Moore. Also check out *Ray Johnson: Correspondences,* edited by Donna De Salvo and Catherine Gudis.

21. Your favorite book.

22. Your favorite album.

23. WhatsYourProject.com. Unique, inventive, and engaging project ideas contributed by people from all over the world. Read them, get inspired, and submit your own project. (This is a component of the *52 Projects* project.)

24. *What Should I Do with My Life?* **by Po Bronson.** Exploration, through the stories and experiences of others, of the biggest dilemma confronting each and every one of us—what in the hell we should do with this incredible life of ours.

25. churchofcraft.org. Community and craft. Not in your town? Start a chapter and put it on the map.

26. *Why Man Creates* **by Saul Bass.** You may have seen this short film in a classroom of long ago on a film projector reel. A truly creative exploration of creativity. Something that has always stuck with me: A scientist explains that the theory he has been doing work on for years is not working out. He seems a bit shell-shocked and despondent. In voiceover as he is walking down a long hallway, and finally out a door, he explains that he doesn't know what he's going to do next.

27. *Journal of a Novel* **by John Steinbeck.** Inside the mind of a writer at work on one of his important works. The journal features letters that Steinbeck wrote to his editor about his writing efforts—both the difficulties and the breakthroughs—each day before he set to work on *East of Eden*.

28. *Writing Down the Bones* by Natalie Goldberg / *The Art of Fiction: Notes on Craft for Young Writers* by John Gardner / *On Writing* by Stephen King / *Burning Down the House: Essays on Fiction* by Charles Baxter / *Bird by Bird: Some Instructions on Writing and Life* by Anne Lamott / *The Forest for the Trees: An Editor's Advice to Writers* by Betsy Lerner.

29. *The Murdering of My Years* by Mickey Z. Interviews with independent project-makers exploring not only how they make their projects, but how they make ends meet as well.

30. The WPA's Federal Writers' Project. (Both the concept and the prolific body of work it created.)

31. Strobelit.com. "Instances of visual interest." Links to cool, inventive, and engaging photography projects, collections, and blogs on the web. Run by Gwen Harlow.

32. 31 Simple Things You Can Do to Get the Word Out About Your Independent Project. At Bookmouth.com. Exactly what it says.

33. Allan Kaprow's *Happenings* art.

34. *Grapefruit* by Yoko Ono.

35. Akira Kurosawa's film *Ikiru* (*see* Project #26).

36. *The New Media Monopoly* by Ben H. Bagdikian. An investigation into media consolidation, with insights into how we are influenced and impacted by the cultural landscape it produces.

37. The lost art of C. Lintero.

38. *Fluxus Codex* by Jon Hendricks / *Fluxus Experience* by Hannah Higgins.

39. Your favorite artist's catalogue *raisonnè*. This will present a comprehensive look at the artist's body of work, and will include descriptions, commentary, time lines, and more.

40. Jim Munroe's NoMediaKings.org. Munroe publishes his own books and makes his own movies. At his website, he shares what he and others have learned so that you, too, can publish your own books and make your own movies.

41. Dave Isay's audio documentary projects, available at soundportraits.org. *See also* StoryCorps.net, a project created to instruct and encourage people to interview each other and record each other's stories in sound.

42. The Special Collections Department at your local or university library. Rare but accessible books and curiosities that have been deemed worthy of extra care and scholarship, all in the hope of keeping the collection preserved and available for the ages.

43. The picture or drawing that has been on your fridge for years.

44. Your favorite quote. (*"This is the true joy in life, the being used for a purpose recognized by yourself as a mighty one . . ."*— George Bernard Shaw, in the "Epistle Dedicatory" to *Man and Superman*.)

45. *Joseph Cornell: Master of Dreams* by Diane Waldman.

46. Street art in your neighborhood. Woostercollective.com (an online showcase of street art). *Subway Art* by Martha Cooper and Henry Chalfant. Also, look for art by Swoon, Shepard Fairey, James De La Vega, and Robbie Conal in a street or alley near you.

47. The one photograph of your significant other that you believe captures him or her perfectly.

48. The artwork you made as a child, saved and safely stored (in the rafters of the garage) by your mother.

49. The wall of family photos in your home/your parent's home/your grandparent's home.

50. The list of people you admire (parents, siblings, high school teachers, coaches, athletes, artists, etc.).

51. The last project you made.

52. Your own personal list of fifty-two inspiration sources. Write it down now.

FOR MORE PROJECTS, AND HOW TO CONTRIBUTE YOUR OWN

THE CREATIVE ENERGY within this book continues on at www.52projects.com. The site is dedicated to thinking outside the craft, and as I'm sure you can guess, it's all about projects and project-making: project ideas, projects to create, projects to check out, and projects to participate in. Writing projects, photo projects, projects, projects, projects. And more projects. Visit the site now and come back regularly (and spell it out as well for access to a secret stash of bonus projects).

Also, this book's focus on projects and project-making begs the question: What's your project? What is that cool thing that you've done, that you do, or have a plan to create? Write it up and send it along. Visit www.whats-yourproject.com for the details. There you will also find the growing number of creative and inspiring projects contributed by project-makers from all over the world.